ILLINOIS
INDIANA
& OHIO
50 HIKES
WITH KIDS

ILLINOIS
INDIANA
& OHIO
50 HIKES
WITH KIDS

SHARON DEWAR
AND WENDY GORTON

Timber Press · Portland, Oregon

Timber Press
Workman Publishing
Hachette Book Group, Inc.
1290 Avenue of the Americas
New York, New York 10104
timberpress.com

Timber Press is an imprint of Workman Publishing, a division of Hachette Book Group, Inc. The Timber Press name and logo are registered trademarks of Hachette Book Group, Inc.

Printed in China on responsibly sourced paper

Series design by Hillary Caudle; layout by Sarah Crumb
Cover design and illustration by Always With Honor
Inside cover map by David Deis

The publisher is not responsible for websites (or their content) that are not owned by the publisher.

The Hachette Speakers Bureau provides a wide range of authors for speaking events. To find out more, go to hachettespeakersbureau.com or email hachettespeakers@hbgusa.com.

ISBN 978-1-64326-164-5

A catalog record for this book is available from the Library of Congress.

To my husband, Alex, for his unwavering support and encouragement; our children, Kaelan and Siena, whose enthusiasm for hiking and nature exploration made this book possible; and my parents, who nurtured a love of nature in me at a young age that shaped my life trajectory.
—SD

==

To Riley, you inspire me everyday to treat every treasure we find outside as a joyful gift, even if it's the 1,000th "munt-noom" (mushroom) we spot.
—WG

CONTENTS

==================================

==================================

PREFACE

Midwesterners, the landscape of Illinois, Indiana, and Ohio are often defined by the richness of their extensive agricultural lands and vibrant cities, but don't underestimate how wild and varied the terrain across these 139,000 square miles really is. As you'll see in this book, there is vast and impressive wilderness—from old-growth forests to deep canyons carved by glaciers, marshes and bald cypress swamps to tallgrass prairies—and ancient preserved cultural history of native peoples who once called this region home. Sometimes the most spectacular terrain is found unexpectedly, surrounded by miles of flat fields that transform into forests with impressive rock ledges, bluffs, and gorges.

Wendy Gorton and Sharon Dewar put this guide together to provide kids of all ages a curated selection of some of the most varied and interesting destinations in Illinois, Indiana, and Ohio. It can reassure busy adults about what to expect from any given trail, the features they will see when they arrive, and the logistics that can make or break an outdoor excursion with kids. There is a focal point of interest for each trail, and all of them are kid-centric hikes. We are excited to share our passion for nature with you.

In 2006, smack in the middle of her second year of teaching fourth graders, Wendy became a PolarTREC GoNorth! teacher explorer. She packed up with a top-notch, experienced adventure crew and set out to spend two weeks dog sledding, interviewing locals about climate change, and collecting snow-pack data. It was the hardest thing she'd ever done to date, but it introduced her to adventure learning, pioneered by the University of Minnesota's Dr. Aaron Doering. Her number-one goal was to interpret the experience for her students back in the classroom and students from around the world who wanted to feel a piece of real-life adventure. Every night, their dogs rushed them through the snow to the next research

Kids enjoy Horseshoe Falls in Ohio

hut in the middle of Finland. Once inside, they peeled off their layers, cooked dinner from their meal rations, used their maps to plan the next day, and got a good night's sleep. Then as now, Wendy studied each day's route with the eyes of a child—finding nooks that delighted her, asking herself big questions, documenting things that interested her but that she couldn't identify on the spot, and researching answers. Many years later, she is thrilled to be creating mini adventures for Midwestern families, helping them to become intrepid adventurers.

Raised in Cincinnati, Sharon has fond childhood memories of tent camping in state parks throughout the Midwest each summer. These early childhood experiences not only inspired her love of the wilderness, but also ignited a sense of curiosity, an adventurous spirit, and a thirst to explore more of the world. She enlisted in the US Navy right after high school graduation and was trained as a journalist and public affairs specialist at Fort Harrison in Indiana. Today, it is no longer a military base, but a state park featured in this book. During her seven years of service, she explored many parts of the world, from climbing Mount Fuji in Japan to exploring the ruins of ancient cultures in Egypt. Since then, she has devoted her career to conservation communications, supporting scientists affiliated with some of the nation's top zoos and environmental organizations, helping them share their research with a wider audience. Her combined passion for nature and journalism has taken her to some of the most remote parts of the planet, from the polar reaches of Svalbard to the deepest forests of the Republic of Congo in search of gorillas and chimpanzees. Her career pursuits and passion for nature were fueled in childhood during those camping trips in the Midwest and while walking in the woods with her parents. She learned not to fear nature, but to find solace, peace, and mental and physical restoration in it. Nature sparks wonder. Now Sharon lives in Oak Park, Illinois, near Chicago, and loves seeing the wonder and awe ignited in her own children as they explore the magnificent natural wonders in this region. Her goal is to help make nature feel welcoming and accessible to everyone.

The driving question behind this book is this: How can we design experiences that inspire wonder in our children? If we—as educators, caregivers, aunties and uncles, grandparents and parents—can provide a fun environment and the initial sparks of curiosity, we can help children discover and explore the world around them, creating a generation of resilient, curious kids who appreciate natural beauty even from a young age. This book is designed to give adults some tools to help ignite questions on the trail, to teach kids that it's great to stop and look at things instead of just rushing from point A to point B, and to begin to introduce a broader understanding of just how many unique places surround us in this Midwestern landscape. By simply venturing out and interacting with kids along the trail, we are building their skills in questioning things they see around them—everywhere—and encouraging them to look for answers.

We hope you get a sense of the love steeped in these pages—the love for outdoors, the love for adventure, the love for planning and preparation, and the love for family and community. Sharon's husband and kids were her co-adventurers on every hike, often squeezing in two to three hikes a day several days in a row to test and find just the right ones for this guide, and choosing which adventures to include was no easy task. The Midwest's number of "kid-friendly" hikes is almost staggering, but we developed a firm Kid Filter of awesome features, simple driving, and turnkey instructions on the trail so you're not second-guessing yourselves and you can simply enjoy time together outdoors immersed in nature.

The benefits of getting children outdoors in nature are extensive. It promotes creativity and imagination, sparks wonder, helps kids focus, builds confidence and critical thinking skills, and reduces stress. Adults also benefit from nature's gifts.

Allison Price, director of learning experiences at Lincoln Park Zoo in Chicago (and mom to Finn and Cameron), likes to remind parents, "Nature has these magical properties. It provides calming, grounding, and balance, which is extremely beneficial. For parents who aren't confident about going out into nature, or who might worry about not knowing the answer to things their child will ask—you don't need to know the answers. Being in nature is about sharing the process of discovery. Being open to new and unknown. Say, 'I don't know, what do you think?' This activates curiosity and whimsy and imagination."

As you romp with your own crew through the outdoors, keep in mind that while the scavenger hunt items called out on each hike might help you add excitement or teachable moments, finding them all should not be the main goal of your outing. We wrote this guide to help you get outside, spend time with your family, and have fun. Allison Price says, "I find it helpful to hike with friends. Having other adults to bond with while our kids play and explore is extra enriching."

Kids lead more structured lives today than ever before. Parents are sometimes pleasantly surprised when they see how much kids enjoy simply being set loose in wide-open spaces. Experiencing the wonders all around us creates lifelong habits of seeking out adventure, appreciating the gifts nature gives us every day, and caring about keeping our natural resources clean, beautiful, and accessible for future generations. All the scaffolds you'll need to plan even more of your own adventures are here.

CHOOSING YOUR ADVENTURE

This guide is designed to help children become co-adventurers with you across the diverse Midwestern landscape, so build excitement by involving them in the planning process from the beginning. Let them flip through and mark the pages they'd like to tackle in the future. Ask them what features they love when they're outside. How hard do they feel like working today for their adventure? How long do they want to hike? The following tables can help you choose. For maximum success with younger kids, no hike is over 5 miles long or gains much more than 1000 feet—perfectly attainable for most little legs. This means that there can be plenty of time for exploration, rest stops, snacks, and just taking in the sights and sounds around you. Have kids help pick hikes for the weekend, slowly but surely checking them all off. We hope you grab a pen and mark all of your achievements throughout the region as your kids grow up, just as you might mark their growing heights on the living room wall.

ADVENTURES IN ILLINOIS

ADVENTURE	CLOSEST CITY	LENGTH (MILES)	DIFFICULTY / ELEVATION (FEET)	HIGHLIGHTS
1 Illinois Beach State Park PAGE 62	Chicago	2	Easy 20'	Beach, rockhounding, oak savannah
2 Moraine Hills State Park PAGE 66	Chicago	3.2	Moderate 105'	Sandhill cranes, threatened aquatic plants
3 Fullersburg Woods PAGE 70	Chicago	2.6	Easy 361'	Creek
4 Little Red Schoolhouse Nature Center PAGE 74	Chicago	2.2	Easy 64'	Nature center, wetlands, birds
5 McKee Marsh PAGE 78	Chicago	2.3	Easy 26'	Wetlands
6 White Pines Forest State Park PAGE 82	Chicago	1.2	Challenging 118'	Old-growth forest, creek crossings
7 Matthiessen State Park PAGE 86	Chicago	1	Moderate 200'	Waterfalls, sandstone bluffs
8 Starved Rock State Park PAGE 90	Chicago	2.3	Moderate 308'	Canyons, creek

ADVENTURE	CLOSEST CITY	LENGTH (MILES)	DIFFICULTY / ELEVATION (FEET)	HIGHLIGHTS
9 Robinson Park *PAGE 94*	Peoria	3.8	Challenging 814'	Flora and fauna, creek crossings
10 Rocky Glen Park *PAGE 98*	Peoria	1.6	Moderate 348'	Box canyon, carvings, historical coal mine
11 Pere Marquette State Park *PAGE 102*	St. Louis	1	Easy 82'	Views, bald eagles
12 Giant City State Park *PAGE 106*	Carbondale	1	Moderate 190'	Rock formations
13 Cache River State Natural Area *PAGE 110*	Harrisburg	3.3	Moderate 85'	Bald cypress trees
14 Bell Smith Springs *PAGE 114*	Harrisburg	2	Moderate 256'	Natural bridge, creek crossing, unique plants
15 Garden of the Gods *PAGE 118*	Harrisburg	2.2	Moderate 223'	Views, ledges and bluffs
16 Rim Rock National Recreational Trail *PAGE 122*	Harrisburg	1.7	Moderate 223'	Ledges and bluffs

ADVENTURES IN INDIANA

ADVENTURE	CLOSEST CITY	LENGTH (MILES)	DIFFICULTY / ELEVATION (FEET)	HIGHLIGHTS
17 Hemlock Cliffs PAGE 128	Louisville	1.5	Moderate 180'	Waterfall
18 Pioneer Mothers Memorial Forest Trail PAGE 132	Louisville	1.5	Easy 125'	Old-growth forest
19 Charlestown State Park PAGE 136	Louisville	2.6	Moderate 360'	Historical ruins
20 Clifty Falls State Park PAGE 140	Madison	1.1	Moderate 266'	Waterfalls
21 Bluffs of Beaver Bend PAGE 144	Louisville	2.9	Moderate 371'	Views
22 Spring Mill State Park PAGE 148	Bloomington	3	Moderate 259'	Caves, sinkholes, old-growth forest
23 Brown County State Park PAGE 152	Bloomington	2.1	Moderate 322'	Views
24 McCormick's Creek State Park PAGE 156	Bloomington	2.5	Moderate 200'	Cave, natural arches, creek crossings
25 Sodalis Nature Park PAGE 160	Indianapolis	2.5	Easy 72'	Rare wildlife

ADVENTURE	CLOSEST CITY	LENGTH (MILES)	DIFFICULTY / ELEVATION (FEET)	HIGHLIGHTS
26 Turkey Run State Park PAGE 164	Indianapolis	1.9	Challenging 394'	Gorges, rare plants
27 Shades State Park PAGE 168	Indianapolis	1.8	Challenging 246'	Waterfall, gorge, rare trees and plants
28 Fort Harrison PAGE 172	Indianapolis	2.8	Challenging 135'	Creeks
29 Potter's Covered Bridge Park PAGE 176	Noblesville	3.2	Easy 30'	River, covered bridge
30 Mounds State Park PAGE 180	Muncie	3	Moderate 144'	River, history, culture,
31 Mississinewa Lake PAGE 184	Peru	2	Moderate 72'	Lake, history
32 Kokiwanee Nature Preserve PAGE 188	Fort Wayne	2	Challenging 118'	Waterfall
33 Lindenwood Nature Preserve PAGE 192	Fort Wayne	2.2	Easy 75'	Stargazing, birds, wildflowers
34 Indiana Dunes National Park PAGE 196	Gary	1.1	Moderate 100'	Dunes

ADVENTURES IN OHIO

ADVENTURE	CLOSEST CITY	LENGTH (MILES)	DIFFICULTY / ELEVATION (FEET)	HIGHLIGHTS
35 Maumee Bay State Park *PAGE 202*	Toledo	1.8	Easy 7'	Wetlands, birds
36 Kelleys Island *PAGE 206*	Lakeside Marblehead	1.5	Easy 23'	Geology, ruins, endangered plants
37 Worden's Ledges *PAGE 210*	Cleveland	1	Easy 92'	Historical carvings
38 Cuyahoga Valley National Park *PAGE 214*	Cleveland	2.3	Moderate 256'	View, ledges
39 Brandywine Falls *PAGE 218*	Cleveland	3.9	Challenging 449'	Waterfall
40 Nelson Kennedy Ledges State Park *PAGE 222*	Cleveland	2	Challenging 148'	Ledges, tunnels, waterfall, rare plants
41 Mill Creek Park *PAGE 226*	Youngstown	2.3	Easy 125'	Waterfall, covered bridge, ledges, historical mill
42 Hocking Hills State Park *PAGE 230*	Columbus	1.2	Moderate 259'	Waterfalls, gorge

ADVENTURE	CLOSEST CITY	LENGTH (MILES)	DIFFICULTY / ELEVATION (FEET)	HIGHLIGHTS
43 **Buzzards Roost Nature Preserve** *PAGE 234*	Chillicothe	2.5	Moderate 290'	View, waterfalls
44 **Englewood MetroPark** *PAGE 238*	Dayton	3.5	Moderate 210'	Waterfalls, rare trees
45 **Glen Helen Nature Preserve** *PAGE 242*	Dayton	1.7	Easy 131'	Waterfalls, burial mound, old-growth trees
46 **Caesar Creek State Park** *PAGE 246*	Lebanon	1.7	Easy 75'	Waterfall, swinging bridge, gorge
47 **Indian Creek MetroPark** *PAGE 250*	Oxford	1.6	Moderate 121'	Creek, burial mound
48 **Sharon Woods** *PAGE 254*	Cincinnati	1.9	Easy 171'	Waterfalls, fitness trail
49 **Bender Mountain Nature Preserve** *PAGE 258*	Cincinnati	2.4	Challenging 390'	Views, birds, rare plants
50 **Serpent Mound** *PAGE 262*	Peebles	1.3	Moderate 121'	Animal effigy mound

Kaelan hikes in
a gorge at Turkey
Run State Park

ADVENTURES BY
FEATURE

Can you remember the first cave you explored? The first waterfall that misted your face? Experiencing hikes that lead to different features will offer children opportunities to explore a variety of natural phenomena and keep them excited for the adventure. Each of the adventures in this guide includes a destination or item of particular interest to motivate young explorers and reward them for their hard work. Encourage children, as co-adventurers, to talk about which types of natural features excite them the most and why.

FEATURE	ADVENTURE
Wetlands, lakes, and ponds	**2** Bog at Moraine Hills State Park
	4 Longjohn Slough at the Little Red Schoolhouse Nature Center
	5 Pond and marsh at McKee Marsh
	13 Pond at Cache River State Natural Area
	25 Pond at Sodalis Nature Park
	31 Lake at Mississinewa Lake
	33 Pond at Lindenwood Nature Preserve
	35 Wetland and swamp at Maumee Bay State Park
	36 Beach at Kelleys Island in Lake Erie
Waterfalls	**7** Lake Falls at Matthiessen State Park
	10 Rocky Glen Falls at Rocky Glen Park
	17 Hemlock Cliffs
	20 Big and Little Clifty Falls
	27 Maidenhair Falls at Shades State Park
	32 Kissing Falls at Kokiwanee Nature Preserve
	39 Brandywine Falls at Cuyahoga Valley National Park
	40 Cascade Falls at Nelson Kennedy Ledges State Park
	41 Lanterman's Falls at Mill Creek Park
	42 Upper and Lower Falls at Hocking Hills State Park
	44 Martindale and Patty Falls at Englewood MetroPark
	45 The Cascades and The Grotto at Glen Helen Nature Reserve
	46 Horseshoe Falls at Caesar Creek State Park
	48 Sharon Creek Falls in Sharon Woods

FEATURE	ADVENTURE
History	**10** Coal mine and historical carvings at Rocky Glen Park
	16 Ancient wall at Rim Rock National Recreational Trail
	18 Memorial at Pioneer Mothers Memorial Forest Trail
	19 Abandoned 1920s amusement park at Rose Island in Charlestown State Park
	22 Pioneer village at Spring Mill State Park
	29 Covered bridge at Potter's Covered Bridge Park
	30 Ancient mounds, and amusement park at Mounds State Park
	36 Ruins from stone crusher factory on Kelleys Island
	37 Historical folk-art stone carvings at Worden's Ledges
	41 Lanterman's Mill and covered bridge at Mill Creek Park
	50 Ancient earthwork effigy at Serpent Mound

FEATURE	ADVENTURE
Flora and Fauna	**2** Leatherleaf ferns and sandhill cranes at Moraine Hills State Park
	4 Ospreys and migrating birds at the Little Red Schoolhouse Nature Center
	6 Old-growth forest at White Pines Forest State Park
	9 Interesting birds and plants at Robinson Park
	11 Bald eagles at Pere Marquette State Park
	13 Bald cypress at Cache River State Natural Area
	14 Rare flowering plants, lichens, and mosses at Bell Smith Springs
	18 Old-growth forest on Pioneer Mothers Memorial Forest Trail
	22 Old-growth forest at Spring Mill State Park
	25 Endangered bats at Sodalis Nature Park
	26 Bryophytes and bald eagles in winter at Turkey Run State Park
	33 Trillium and wild ginger at Lindenwood Nature Preserve
	35 Birds and reptiles at Maumee Bay State Park
	36 Lakeside daisies on Kelleys Island
	40 Red trillium and yellow birch at Nelson Kennedy Ledges State Park
	44 Rare pumpkin ash trees at Englewood MetroPark
	49 Rare wildflowers at Bender Mountain Nature Preserve

FEATURE	ADVENTURE
Geology	**7** Sandstone bluffs at Matthiessen State Park
	10 Box canyon at Rocky Glen Park
	12 Balanced Rock and giant stone formations at Giant City State Park
	14 Natural stone arch at Bell Smith Springs
	15 Indian Point at Garden of the Gods
	16 Ox-Lot Cave on Rim Rock National Recreational Trail
	17 Rock ledges at Hemlock Cliffs
	21 Mansfield Sandstone at Bluffs of Beaver Bend
	22 Sinkholes, caves, and sinking streams at Spring Mill State Park
	24 Wolf Cave at McCormick's Creek State Park
	26 Glacial potholes and gorges at Turkey Run State Park
	27 Steamboat Rock and Pearl Ravine at Shades State Park
	30 Seeps and springs at Mounds State Park
	36 Glacial grooves on Kelleys Island
	38 Ice Box Cave and Sharon Sandstone and Conglomerate at Cuyahoga Valley National Park
	40 Sharon Conglomerate, The Squeeze, Fat Man's Peril, and Devil's Icebox at Nelson Kennedy Ledges State Park
	42 Devil's Bathtub, Old Man's Cave, and Black Hand Sandstone at Hocking Hills State Park
	45 Yellow Springs at Glen Helen Nature Preserve

FEATURE	ADVENTURE
Overlooks and peaks	**11** McAdam's Peak at Pere Marquette State Park
	15 Indian Point at Garden of the Gods
	21 Bluffs of Beaver Bend
	23 Lookout shelter on Trail 2 at Brown County State Park
	38 Ledges Trail at Cuyahoga Valley National Park
	43 Buzzards Roost at Buzzards Roost Nature Preserve
	49 Ridgeline at Bender Mountain
Rivers and creeks	**6** Spring and Pine Creeks at White Pines Forest State Park
	7 Stream from Matthiessen's Lake in Matthiessen State Park
	14 Bay Creek at Bell Smith Springs
	26 Rocky Hollow Stream at Turkey Run State Park
	27 Sugar Creek at Shades State Park
	28 Camp and Falls Creeks at Fort Harrison
	29 White River along Potter's Covered Bridge Park
	39 Brandywine Creek at Cuyahoga Valley National Park
	41 Mill Creek at Mill Creek Park
	47 Indian Creek at Indian Creek MetroPark
	50 Ohio Brush Creek at Serpent Mound
Beach fun	**1** Illinois Beach State Park
	31 Mississinewa Lake
	34 Indiana Dunes National Park
	36 Kelleys Island

FEATURE	ADVENTURE
Campground by trailhead	**1** Illinois Beach State Park Campground
	4 Camp Bullfrog Lake near the Little Red Schoolhouse Nature Center
	5 Blackwell Family Campground near McKee Marsh
	6 Sunny Crest Family Campground near White Pines Forest State Park
	7 Cozy Corners Campground near Matthiessen State Park
	8 Starved Rock State Park Campground
	11 Class A/B Campgrounds at Pere Marquette State Park
	12 Giant City State Park Campground
	13 Shawnee Forest Campground near Cache River State Natural Area
	14 Redbud Campground at Bell Smith Springs
	15 Pharaoh Campground near Garden of the Gods
	16 Double M Campground near Rim Rock National Recreational Trail
	17 Indian-Celina Lakes Recreational Area near Hemlock Cliffs
	18 Sleeping Bear Retreat near Pioneer Mothers Memorial Forest Trail
	19 Charlestown State Park Campground
	20 Clifty Falls Campground
	21 Martin State Forest Campground near Bluffs of Beaver Bend
	22 Spring Mill State Park Campground
	23 Buffalo Ridge Campground at Brown County State Park
	24 McCormick's Creek State Park Campground

FEATURE	ADVENTURE
Campground by trailhead (cont'd)	**26** Turkey Run State Park Campground
	27 Shades State Park Campground
	29 White River Campground at Potter's Covered Bridge Park
	30 Mounds State Park Campground
	31 Mississinewa Lake State Park Campground
	32 Salamonie River State Forest Family Campground
	34 Dunewood Campground at Indiana Dunes National Park
	36 Kelleys Island State Park Campground
	38 Ottawa Overlook Backcountry Sites near Cuyahoga Valley National Park
	40 Nelson Ledges Quarry Park Campground near Nelson-Kennedy Ledges State Park
	42 Hocking Hills State Park Campground
	43 Shawnee Valley Campground near Buzzards Roost Nature Preserve
	44 Patty Hollow Campground at Englewood MetroPark
	45 John Bryan State Park Campground near Glen Helen Nature Preserve
	46 Caesar Creek State Campground

ADVENTURES BY SEASON

Many trails are available year-round for your adventuring pleasure, yet some really sing during particular moments of the year, so prepare your family to be ready for any season. Spring is often great for wildflower blooms or trails with waterfalls at maximum flow, but for some trails it's mud season—check conditions beforehand (and make sure the trail isn't closed), plan footwear, and consider a hiking stick or trekking poles. Summer allows the best access to more exposed, rocky trails that might be slippery or treacherous during winter, but the season also comes with copious mosquitoes, flies, and ticks—bring repellent and always do checks. In fall, many trails erupt with color and mushrooms, but some trails go near areas that allow hunting—always check the signs and consider bringing orange shirts and hats in your adventure bag. Winter can be a great time to escape crowds, especially if you bring your snowshoes or ice tracks. Always check the forecast and road conditions before venturing out in winter months, and consider checking AllTrails.com for recent trip reports to see if trails are packed down and safe. Keep in mind that any prime season means you might encounter crowds, so consider visiting early or late in the day, or try exploring during an off-season. Help your kids to understand the seasons by returning to a favorite hike throughout the year and asking them what's changed since their last visit.

Fall is a favorite for many families
in the Midwest

PEAK SEASON	ADVENTURE
Winter	**5** McKee Marsh
	11 Pere Marquette State Park
	12 Giant City State Park
	21 Bluffs of Beaver Bend
	22 Spring Mill State Park
	33 Lindenwood Nature Preserve
	40 Nelson Kennedy Ledges State Park
	43 Buzzards Roost Nature Preserve
Spring	**3** Fullersburg Woods
	8 Starved Rock State Park
	10 Rocky Glen Park
	14 Bell Smith Springs
	16 Rim Rock National Recreational Trail
	17 Hemlock Cliffs
	19 Charlestown State Park
	20 Clifty Falls State Park
	28 Fort Harrison
	32 Kokiwanee Nature Preserve
	34 Indiana Dunes National Park
	35 Maumee Bay State Park
	39 Brandywine Falls
	42 Hocking Hills State Park
	45 Glen Helen Nature Preserve
	49 Bender Mountain

PEAK SEASON	ADVENTURE
Summer	**1** Illinois Beach State Park
	4 The Little Red Schoolhouse Nature Center
	6 White Pines Forest State Park
	7 Matthiessen State Park
	13 Cache River State Natural Area
	24 McCormick's Creek State Park
	25 Sodalis Nature Park
	26 Turkey Run State Park
	27 Shades State Park
	31 Mississinewa Lake
	36 Kelleys Island
	38 Cuyahoga Valley State Park
	44 Englewood MetroPark
	47 Indian Creek MetroPark
	50 Serpent Mound
Fall	**2** Moraine Hills State Park
	9 Robinson Park
	15 Garden of the Gods
	18 Pioneer Mothers Memorial Forest Trail
	23 Brown County State Park
	29 Potter's Covered Bridge Park
	30 Mounds State Park
	37 Worden's Ledges
	41 Mill Creek Park
	46 Caesar Creek State Park
	48 Sharon Woods

PREPARING FOR YOUR ADVENTURE

This guide is a starter pack to a life full of adventure with your young ones. One day, your adventurers could be calling you up to ask if you want to trek the Appalachian Trail together. Both authors' own parents instilled a love of nature in us and inspired our thirst for outdoor adventure, and today, we're passing that on, bringing family with us on all the hikes in this guide. We hope you'll work together to taste what each spectacularly diverse region has to offer and note which you'd like to return to in the future. The guide is organized by state—we'll start off in Illinois, explore Indiana, and work our way east to Ohio.

INDIVIDUAL ADVENTURE PROFILES

Each of the fifty adventure profiles includes a basic trail map and information on the species of plants and wildlife, points of historical interest, and geological features that you may see on the trail. Allowing children to navigate using the maps and elevation guides, reading the hike and species descriptions, and looking for each featured item in the scavenger hunts puts the building blocks of adventure in their hands. Marking journeys on the map with points of interest gives relevance and context to kids' surroundings, so encourage them to note anything that stood out to them, even if it's not noted in the book. You'll burst with pride when kids start to teach you what a lollipop loop is versus an out and back, gauge whether they feel like just kickin' it on a hike with 200 feet of elevation gain or tackling 800 feet, and make decisions about their own adventure. Each description is written for both you and the kids, so encourage them to read to themselves or out loud to you.

Elevation profile, length, type of trail, and time

The elevation profile graph is a line that sketches the general arch of the up-and-down during the hike. You'll notice that many are almost completely flat, and some are nearly a triangle. The elevation listed is how many feet you'll gain from start to finish; so even if it rolls up and then down again, if it says 300 feet, that will be the total number of feet you'll gain from the trailhead to the highest point. No adventure is less than 1 mile, which we feel is too short to call a real excursion, or more than 5 miles, which might make it inaccessible for many of our younger or newer adventurers. The length of these hikes should give you plenty of time to enjoy the outing before anyone gets too tired. Embracing shorter trails translates into more time to savor them. Some of the routes are shorter versions of a longer or different route and are modified for kids. Along with the length of the trail, we note whether the adventure is an out and back, a loop, or a lollipop loop, and whether a clockwise or counterclockwise route is recommended.

An out and back has a clear final destination and turnaround point, and you'll cross back over what you've already discovered.

A loop provides brand-new territory the whole way around.

A lollipop is a straight line with a mini loop at the end, like reaching a lake, then circling it and heading back.

There are variations on these basic shapes, like a figure eight or a Y-shaped out and back, and discussing shape classification can be a fun way to get kids thinking about the route. Talking about the type of trail you're planning to hike helps young adventurers know what to expect. The estimated hike time includes time for exploration, but each adventurer's mileage may vary. Always give yourselves the delight of a relaxing hike with plenty of time to stop and play with a pile of fun-looking rocks, have leaf-boat races on a stream, or sketch a cool plant or animal in a nature journal.

Waterfalls are points of interest on several hikes

Level of difficulty

Often, when you research "kid-friendly" hikes, you'll find relatively sterile, flat, paved trails. While these are perfect for first-time hikers or toddlers, we know kids are capable of more, so the hikes in this book are all true-blue hikes and adventures. It's important to note that these are kid-centric ratings; what's labeled as a "challenging" trail in this guide may not appear to be so challenging for a seasoned adult hiker. It can be fun to create your own rating for a trail when

Overlooks can provide a sense of accomplishment for your young adventurers

you're finished. "Did that feel like a level one, two, or three to you? Why?" Talking about it can help you understand an individual kid's adventure limits or help them seek new challenges. There will be notes if a trail has exposed ledges or viewpoints where you'll want to hold small hands. Rocky terrain begs for sturdy shoes, and you'll want to have an idea about how wet, muddy, or snowy it may be to choose which pair will be best for your child. It can help if you check reviews on AllTrails.com to get recent conditions and different families' opinions of the difficulty—you can also call the office of a nearby ranger station. While scouting these trails with our families, we saw many walking toddlers, strollers of every tire type imaginable, and baby backpacks on even the most challenging trails. We also spotted a couple of sport strollers on moderately rocky trails with exposed roots. Use the information here to make informed decisions—every lead adventurer is different.

The adventures are rated as follows:

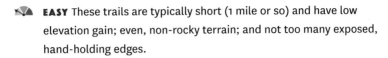 **EASY** These trails are typically short (1 mile or so) and have low elevation gain; even, non-rocky terrain; and not too many exposed, hand-holding edges.

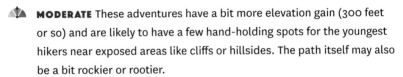 **MODERATE** These adventures have a bit more elevation gain (300 feet or so) and are likely to have a few hand-holding spots for the youngest hikers near exposed areas like cliffs or hillsides. The path itself may also be a bit rockier or rootier.

CHALLENGING These will give your little adventurers the biggest sense of accomplishment. They have the most elevation gain (300 to 800 feet) and include sections where you'll probably want kids to stay close as they take in an exposed view. However, if the trail is steeper, it'll also be shorter—more than doable with the right attitude and by taking advantage of power-up stops and the adrenaline-inducing rush of finding special scavenger hunt items.

Season

This section lists the season when the adventure is possible; in many cases, trails can be hiked year round. We also note the seasons when features of special interest can be seen, such as wildflowers or rushing waterfalls. Phenology is the study of how plants change across the seasons, and hikers are often the first to notice when leaves change colors or when a certain flower starts to bloom. Try taking the same hike in several seasons to teach your little adventurers about differences in the seasons, particularly for flora and fauna. The more often you go, the more likely you are to find something you may have missed the last time.

In winter and early spring, check with the local agency listed for each hike to make sure the trail and access road is actually open. In general, hikes near water features, like streams and rivers, are more likely to be

Midwest seasons are vastly different and we love to hike during them all! Winter in the Ohio Valley appears quite drab and dead at first glance, but getting out in the woods and hiking allows us to see the surprise glimpses of color hidden in gray rocks and bare branches, enjoy the varied light perspective from the lower sun angle, and observe the unique distinctions in nature that go beyond the more obvious leaves and flowers. I love how our family gets a richer understanding of our environment during that wintry season of preparation!

—Laura Tolbert, Indiana mother of seven who is preparing to thru-hike the Appalachian Trail in 2025

closed by high water or ice on either side of summer. Some adventures lend themselves to snow exploration without any gear, while others provide an opportunity to try snowshoes or ice tracks.

Get there

When Wendy was seven, her dad took her family out for their first off-roading experience in a small white Toyota pickup in the California desert. Their truck was promptly lodged between two rocks and got towed out six hours later. Although that experience built some character and an adventurous spirit in her, these kinds of roads are not included in this guide. These adventures have all been road-tested at least once and specifically target trailheads with fairly easy access, meaning minimal dirt, gravel, or pothole-strewn roads. We'll leave those to our seasoned adventurers.

We'll be covering a lot of ground throughout Illinois, Indiana, and Ohio—over 139,000 square miles. This guide is meant to be a promotion for the diverse and beautiful areas all over the region. We hope that you and your children flip through and dream of one day taking a road trip to the most southern point of Illinois, experiencing bald cypress swamps reminiscent of the bayous of Louisiana, or taking a ferry to a blissfully quiet beach on Kelleys Island.

Crossing a ford at White Pines Forest State Park

Car rides are a necessity to reach this amazing buffet of hikes available to you, Midwesterners, and we hope you embrace the special family time that road trips can offer your crew. Of course, you have your screen of choice, but consider a few fun ways to make the hours fly by fast, such as riddles, the A–Z game (you claim a point every time you see something that starts with the next letter of the alphabet), audiobooks, call-and-response-type camp songs (ultimatecampresource.com/camp-songs), nature journaling, and just good old-fashioned conversation. Always be ready to roll down windows for fresh air and encourage your little riders to look at the horizon if they start to get carsick. Oftentimes, we've sent you to a verified awesome spot in the midst of even more to explore. We encourage you to always stop by visitor centers, make the most of every trip, and consider finding somewhere nearby to camp to enjoy the area longer.

Basic directions to the trailhead are listed with each adventure, along with a *case-sensitive* Google Maps link you can drop directly into your smartphone browser. Be sure to do this before you head out, while you're certain to have coverage. You can also get free highway maps mailed to you or printed, which can be helpful and educational for your little copilot (check the tourism website for each state). Before leaving home, you and your adventurer can geek out on Google Earth or turn on satellite view in Google Maps to follow your route (and sometimes even your trail) step by step.

There's something magical about maps, and each map in this guide was carefully designed with kids in mind, for them to touch, trace, and hold out in front of them to understand their surroundings. Encourage your kids to understand the difference between roads, highways, and interstate freeways. We've simplified the maps so kids can focus on the land agencies they'll be visiting, the closest towns with grub stops, and the larger adventure hub cities nearby. Hopefully, while they adventure with you, they'll start to build a sixth sense for using maps. Ask them navigation questions. *How long will this adventure take, do you think? Where does that river start, and how is it related to the ocean? How many turns will we need to make? What's our next highway? Any cities nearby? Any fun names you can see?* Just asking questions can encourage curiosity and leadership in your young adventurers.

Trail blazes

Keep a keen eye on the trail and map because trail blazes guide the way on almost every trail. While Sharon and Wendy have made every effort to pick trails that are straightforward and hard to get lost on, it's a good habit to have your children always looking for the next blaze. They should question if they haven't seen one in a few minutes, take note of the landmarks around them at each power-up, and know what the next landmark is on the map. It can be a coveted role to be the first person to see each blaze. These skills will help kids out for more difficult trails when they get older and graduate from this guide. Give a hug to one of the trees with blazes to send a mental thank you to the land agencies who maintain them and make outdoor adventure possible for us all.

Restrooms

We can't have a hiking book for kids without chatting about restrooms. Many trails have pit toilets or developed toilets right at the parking lot. If not, plan on a restroom stop in the nearest town or gas station on your way in and out. Discuss appropriate trail restroom etiquette with your kids as well, such as heading safely off the trail, away from water, and properly covering it should the need arise. Pack your adventure bag with what you need to be comfortable, such as a zip-top baggie with toilet paper. Don't leave any

Look for trail blazes to stay on the correct path

toilet paper behind to spoil some-one else's experience; make sure to pack it back out.

Parking and fees

Your main goal, lead adventurers, is to get out on the trail. If thinking about how to park and pay gets your boot laces knotted up, rest assured that as long as you have some cash and a credit card in the glove compartment, the team will be just fine. All the trailheads listed here have a parking lot or pull-out and some sort of trail sign indicating where you are and whether you need a parking pass or permit. Many of the hikes featured require no fees. Ohio and Illinois state parks are free to access, as is Cuyahoga Valley National Park in Ohio. Some metro parks and private reserves require passes or permits, and some have varied fees between in-state residents or out-of-state visitors. Indiana State Parks offers day fees and annual passes—and if you're wondering whether these passes are worth it, they most certainly are. We have witnessed firsthand how safe and well-maintained the staff and rangers keep trails for us and our families, and these fees pay for that maintenance.

Treat yourself

The guide lists nearby cafés and restaurants for good, quick bites to reward yourselves, in part so you can plan whether you need to pack substantial snacks or just a few for sustenance on the trail. These are road-tested

Kaelan powers up with ice cream after a long hike

bakeries, ice cream shops, burger joints, and family-friendly breweries with notable items or spaces that your kids will enjoy.

Managing agencies

We've listed the name of the agency that manages each hiking trail, along with its telephone number and pertinent social media handles. Before heading out, it's a good idea to check on current conditions, including weather, roads, wildlife sightings, and any hazards that haven't been cleared or fixed. The folks on the other end are often rangers and are generally thrilled to share information about their trails. They can also connect you to botanists, geologists, historians, and other experts. We received fast and enthusiastic responses from many of the rangers behind the Facebook pages of these parks—involve your kids and encourage them to say hello and ask about conditions or a lingering question from the trail.

Scavenger hunts

The scavenger hunt included with each adventure invites you to look for specific fungi, plants, animals, geology, and historical items of interest. You'll find descriptions and photos of trees, leaves, flowers, seeds, cones, bark, nuts, wildlife or animal tracks, fur and feathers, rocks and geological features, historically significant landmarks or artifacts, natural features such as lakes, rivers, and waterfalls, or culturally significant spots that appear on each trail. Entries have questions to ponder or activities to try, and, when applicable, you can dig into the scientific genus and species and learn why a plant or animal is called what it is. Encourage kids to "preview" what they might see on the trail, and if they think they've found it, pull out the book to match. Take it up a notch and encourage them to make their *own* scavenger hunt—write down five things they think they might see on the trail today, from very basic (at least five trees) to very specific (five Eastern white pine cones on the ground).

IDENTIFYING WHAT YOU FIND

When I was about 12 years old my friend and I found what we were sure was a bone from some large extinct animal. My mom drove us down to the Orton Geological Museum at Ohio State, with our earth-shattering discovery carefully wrapped and placed in a cardboard box. It was a big let-down to learn it was just a piece of chert (flint). It's all about education, and you can learn from each find and sharpen your knowledge and skills at identification. This can lead to a rewarding hobby as a collector or maybe even to a career as a museum curator!

—Dave Dyer, Curator of Natural History, Ohio History Collection

The Midwest is covered with forests, prairies, and wetlands full of plants, fungi, mammals, birds, invertebrates, reptiles and amphibians—and fossils! It is also rich with ancient cultures, featuring many earthworks from native people who lived here thousands of years ago. Identifying burial mounds or species in the wild involves using clues from the shape and structure of the landscape, or the size of leaves, bark, flowers, and the habitat. Work with kids to ask questions that will move them from general identification (Is it a conifer/evergreen or a deciduous tree?) to specifics (What shape are the leaves? What species is this?). The species of trees, shrubs, mushrooms, wildflowers, and animals listed in the scavenger hunts were chosen because

Kaelan finds a beaver lodge along the trail

you should be able to find them with ease, and because there's something interesting about them that might appeal to children. You may not find every species on the trail every time, however. It's best to adopt the attitude of considering it a win when you do find one, and to present those you can't find as something to look forward to next time.

Tristan Gooley, British author of *The Natural Navigator*, encourages kids to look for "keys" as they walk on trails. "Keys are small families of clues and signs, if we focus on them repeatedly, it can give us a sixth sense." Start noticing where the sun is when you start and end, and where the natural features (hills, mountains) are around you. Use a compass (there's probably one on your smartphone) to start understanding direction and building this natural sixth sense Gooley speaks of.

When you find a particularly interesting species that's not mentioned in the scavenger hunt, have kids either sketch it or take a photo of it. Remind them to look it up later, either in a printed field guide to the region

Kids love being able to use phones to identify the treasures on the trail

or on a specialty website such as wildflowersearch.com or iNaturalist.org. Including basic descriptions and the name of the region in the search will help kids find their treasure in online field guides. The apps LeafSnap and Seek are also great for creating species treasure hunts on the trail.

Chris Benda, botanist with Southern Illinois University, suggests asking kids questions as they are observing plants to help them develop skills for identification. "What is the leaf arrangement? Is it opposite, alternate, or whorled? Does it have hairs? If so, are they on the stem or the leaf? One side or both sides? These are helpful clues. There is so much variety and unique plants to discover. Before I moved to Illinois I thought of it as mainly corn fields. I was blown away by what is here. I honestly think people have no idea of the richness of Illinois—it's utterly priceless and magnificent!"

If you're ready to level up everyone's identification skills, join the Native Plant Trust or each state's native plant society or botanical society. All have great Facebook groups, newsletters, and online forums where

Check out how the Wisconsinan glacier left behind these grooves on Kelleys Island

you can share when species start to bloom or a photo of a species you can't identify. Be sure to check out program offerings at the forest preserves, state parks, nature preserves, and metro parks, as many offer great family-friendly programs and group hikes, with themes from wildflowers to fungi and everything in between. These programs expose kids to the power of a community resource where everyone is passionate about nature and science and wants to help one another. The USA Phenology Network (usanpn.org) allows kids to contribute to actual science by entering their observation of seasonal changes into a nationwide database, and it has a cool Junior Phenologist program, plus kid-friendly resources to boot.

Illinois, Indiana, and Ohio's geography and geology was shaped by glaciers—the last ice sheet receded about 20,000 to 12,000 years ago. "We have a glacial history similar to Illinois and Ohio. Two-thirds of Indiana is covered with glacial materials, leaving only the south-central part of the state unglaciated. The several glaciers that crossed Indiana covered the relief left from 300 million years of erosion. Every time glaciers came down from the north and northeast, they would bulldoze down highs and fill in lows," explains Todd Thompson, Ph.D., Indiana state geologist. "Most people think of this region as flat cropland, but there is a lot of diverse topography here, from high coastal dunes and relic shorelines to glacial moraines, eroded canyons, waterfalls, and dimpled karst terrains. The Knobstone Escarpment stretching from Louisville to Brown County has exposed rocks with 300-foot relief."

This region is a very cool place to explore rocks and geology, and you'll notice some amazing sights in the adventures. When encountering these gorges, glacial potholes, rock ledges, and fossil-filled bedrock, encourage children to think about the general rock cycle—a rock's evolution from igneous to metamorphic to sedimentary—and how it builds up in deposits over time. Use the scavenger hunts to start to build a familiarity with sandstone ledges and glacial erratic boulders, so your kids can start to find them and notice the subtle differences. Ask questions: What does the texture of the rock look and feel like? What color is it? Does it feel heavy or light? Is it hard or soft? Does it break easily? Join a regional geological society like the Ohio Geological Society (ohiogeosoc.org) and the Midwest Federation of Mineralogical and Geological Societies (mwfed.org) for newsletters, group hikes, and community opportunities. You can even join the National Speleological Society if you're interested in caves.

HISTORICAL ITEMS

This region has rich human history and several sacred sites that offer opportunities to connect with nature and cultural learning about ancestral Native Americans. From the UNESCO World Heritage Site Cahokia Mounds in Southern Illinois, to Mounds State Park in Indiana, to the Serpent Mound in Ohio—and many more sacred sites throughout these states—there are opportunities to engage kids in history and the heritage of these lands.

According to Brad Lepper, Senior Archaeologist with Ohio History Connection, "Indigenous people created monumental earthen architecture that incorporated in its design and construction a deep knowledge of geometry and astronomy, and it's likely that these great earthworks were pilgrimage centers to which people brought offerings of precious items from their homelands. I think it is really

An 1827 map of Illinois, Indiana, and Ohio

important to engage kids with cultural history and learning. Visit these sites and ground their knowledge and experience about these sacred places to create deeper understanding and appreciation for the sophisticated societies of ancient Native Americans who created them."

Jill Weiss Simins, a historian with the Indiana Historical Bureau, says, "The region is a story of migration, and travel routes and settlements. Many cultures overlap and there is great diversity here that is often underestimated." Join your local historical society to start to identify items of historical interest on Illinois, Indiana, and Ohio trails. Each state has its own historical society with resources and an email and phone number to ask questions: Ohio History Connection (ohiohistory.org), Indiana Historical Society (indianahistory.org) and Illinois State Historical Society (historyillinois.org).

Weiss Simins also encourages parents to foster inquiry with each hike: "When you are out in nature at these sites, just pause and ask questions. Who was here before me? What was important to them and what we can learn from them? This kind of inquiry is the most relevant thing because it's how kids learn to become engaged citizens by understanding the layers of history at these sites and the people who came before them. You don't have to memorize facts. You can get kids engaged in history through exploration."

POWER-UP STOPS

Liz Thomas has hiked over 20,000 miles and is a former speed record holder for the Appalachian Trail. Her biggest tip for young adventurers learning to build stamina is: "Understand your body. Kids are just figuring out how to read their bodies. You can think of your body as having gauges and you're the pilot at the front of the plane. Your goal is to keep your gauges (hydration, exposure, food) in the happy zone." She even sets reminders on her watch to drink and eat as she walks from sunrise to sunset. As lead adventurers, you'll be keeping a close eye on these gauges but also helping kids recognize, anticipate, and power through them.

For each adventure, we note key places that serve as mini milestones, or power-up stops. Be sure to pack snacks for kids to eat at these stops to keep blood sugar and energy levels up, and mood high. Remember that this amount of physical activity may be challenging for littles. Often, these power-up stops are at points of interest: fun bridges, switchbacks before a small hill, or viewpoint overlooks. Stopping for a moment can fuel you up, give you a chance to listen to the wind or animals around you, watch what's going on in the woods, and prepare you for the larger goal of finishing the adventure itself.

Power-ups can also be great for a nursing mom or bottle-feeding parent, or for tending to other little ones' needs, as well as for question-based games like I Spy. As the lead adventurer, you can use these stops

Overlooks make great stops to just relax and explore

for inspiration, play, questions, games, and riddles. Encourage your kids to do the same. Don't underestimate the power of choosing a special snack to serve as a particular motivator on tough ascents or rainy days. Indiana mom Laura Tolbert told us, "I'm frequently surprised at how much food the kids consume on the trail, especially in cooler weather! We prefer to have enough with us so that we can take a snack break at least every hour or mile."

ADVENTURE BAG, SUPPLIES, AND SAFETY

Start your kids on a lifelong habit of packing an adventure bag, whether it's the smallest satchel or the largest consumer-grade backpack they can hold. The art of having everything you need with you, without being too burdened, is key to having a good time on the trail. All of these adventures are short enough that even if you did pack too much, the weight won't jeopardize your enjoyment levels too heavily. Review the trail location, its length, and proximity to town, and decide what your team needs to feel comfortable and safe.

- **NAVIGATION** In addition to the maps in this book, consider investing in a compass and full trail map of the area. Make sure your smartphone is fully charged, with offline maps available and the compass feature handy. Our families like to carry portable batteries for phones.

- **HYDRATION** Bring plenty of water for everyone, and remember to drink along the way.

- **NUTRITION** Consider the length of the trail and the amount and type of snacks you'll need to keep the train going.

- **FIRE** Pack a lighter or matchbook for emergencies.

- **FIRST AID KIT** This can range from a mini first aid kit with essentials such as bandages and aspirin to much heftier options with space blankets. Consider what you want your car stocked with and what you want on the trail with you.

- **TOOLS** A small knife or multi-tool goes a long way in the woods.

- **ILLUMINATION** Did you explore just a wee bit too long and dusk is approaching? A simple headlamp, flashlight, or even your phone's flashlight can help lead the way.

- **SUN AND INSECT PROTECTION** If it's an exposed trail, consider sunglasses and sunscreen or hats for you and the kids. In summer and when things get warm, many trails may have mosquitoes, flies, and ticks, so be prepared with your favorite method of repelling them.

- **SHELTER** You may want a space blanket or small tarp in your adventure bag in case of emergency.

- **INSULATION** Check the weather together and decide the type of protection and warmth you want to bring. A second layer is always a good idea—breezes can chill even the warmest of days.

Other fun items to have on hand might include a nature journal and pen or pencil, hand lens, binoculars, a bug jar for capturing and releasing spiders and insects, a camera, a super-special treat for when you reach the top of something, a container for a specimen you find—*if* it's okay with the land agency you're on to collect it—and even a favorite figurine or toy that your littles are currently enamored with, which they can use to interact with that tree stump up ahead. Wet wipes, toilet paper, and zip-top baggies are also recommended. First-timer? Join the local chapter of a hiking group like Outgrown (formerly Hike it Baby), Forest Trails Hiking Club, Hoosiers Hiking Council, or Central Ohio Hiking Club to hike with your peers and learn the ropes of packing.

Lenore Skenazy, president of Let Grow (a nonprofit promoting independence as a critical part of childhood) and founder of the Free-Range Kids movement, understands you might be nervous about shepherding your family into the unknown. She says: "I'm often asked, 'What if something goes wrong?' I love to ask back, 'Can you remember something that went wrong when you were a kid, playing with other kids?' People often look back so fondly on that time when things went wrong. There's even a word for the way we treasure imperfect things and moments: *wabi sabi* ... because the imperfection is what makes it beautiful. The outdoors is never without some surprises and even minor risks, but neither is the indoors. My guess is all adults can remember when something went wrong and it's a treasured (if only in retrospect) memory. Imperfection is inevitable and valuable. Embrace it!"

While it may be handy for you to navigate to each trailhead using your smartphone, remember that many of these wilderness areas have spotty cell service. As a general safety practice for hiking with kids, always tell a third party where you are going and when you expect to be back, and remember to tell anyone who may need to get a hold of you while you're away that you're not certain of cell coverage in the area. On the trail itself, every lead adventurer will have their own comfort level with

Binoculars can enhance the wildlife viewing experience

Our must-haves on the trail include plenty of water and snacks, and a basic first aid kit with antiseptic wipes, bandages, tweezers, and bug sting wipes. We always have a map—even if the trail is easy to follow, my kids love using it to track our progress. Extra socks and pants in case someone ends up falling in the mud or stepping too deep in a creek. Basic extra clothes can save the day. Sunscreen, bug spray, hats, hand wipes, and a zip-top baggie (for trash, muddy clothes, leaves collected from the ground—we always seem to need one), and a lint roller (I leave it in the car, but it has saved the day when dealing with a nest of seed ticks!) Finally, a small, cheap camera— the kids love taking their own pictures while exploring."
—Sara Lesire, St. Louis–region mom

safety, and you'll determine when your children will need hand-holding or reminders to stay close as you get near tricky terrain, exposed edges, or water. Adverse weather conditions can sometimes arrive seemingly out of nowhere. Teaching awareness and common sense, and fostering an attitude of "there's no bad weather, only the wrong clothing," in these situations will go a long way toward creating an adventurous and resilient child. You can model this "love the unlovable" attitude by remaining upbeat and playful as lead adventurer, and you'll be amazed at how quickly their attention will turn back to the trail and its wonders.

Poison ivy is a common hazard lurking across the Midwest, and you'll soon be able to spot it like infrared vision on the trail once you can identify it. Touching this plant will cause a blistering rash in most people. Teach your kids the rhyme "leaves of three, leave it be." The leaves are usually red in spring, green in summer, yellow-orange in fall, and bright red in winter before they shrivel up and fall off. Timber rattlesnakes (*Crotalus horridus*), copperheads (*Agkistrodon contortrix*), and cottonmouths (*Agkistrodon piscivorus*) are three other hazards that come with the call of adventure. Venomous snakes are not common on the trails, and they will not want to bother you, but it is important to be vigilant. If you spot a snake, give a wide berth as you walk around it, and don't poke your hands into rocks or under logs. By helping kids be aware on the trail—looking for signs of wildlife and knowing what to do when they come across it—you can create a lifelong safety skill set for adventuring. Please be aware that some trails close to hikers periodically in fall and winter if they open for hunting; they also sometimes close during spring or winter due to high water or poor weather conditions. It's always a good idea to check the managing agency website or Facebook pages before you set out.

Poison ivy (*Toxicodendron radicans*)

In the Midwest, ticks, tick-borne diseases, and tick prevention and safety is essential and goes hand in hand with hiking. Ticks don't fly or jump; they attach to animals that come into direct contact with them, then they feed on the blood (yours, your dog's, other mammals). They love shrubby, grassy areas—be sure to stick to the center of the trail

Ticks are small, so be sure to check for them carefully

and don't go off-trail. Before a hike, consider wearing light clothing so you can quickly spot any ticks that have hitched a ride. Consider treating your clothes with 0.5 percent permethrin or 20–30 percent DEET (be sure to apply for your children, avoiding eyes, nose, and mouth). Make full-body tick checks a part of your hiking routine when you get back to the car. Be sure to check under your arms, behind your knees and ears, and between your toes. Shower or bath time at home provides another chance for a full-body check. If you find a tick, remove it with tweezers or a tick removal kit as close to your skin as possible. Don't handle it with your bare hands. Clean the area with soap and water, and call your doctor. Ticks can be found in almost any season, so it's best to always perform checks.

NATURE JOURNALING

Wendy received her first nature journal in Sydney, Australia, on her first night as a National Geographic Fellow with a group of students and teachers from around the world. It was leather bound and bursting with empty pages just begging to be doodled and documented on (she now has six and counting). Catherine Hughes, retired head of the National Geographic Kids magazine education team, provided these key maxims for nature journaling:

Siena does rubbings of the leaves collected from the ground on the trail

❁ **Make quick, messy field notes.** You can add details later when you have free time, like during the drive home. You don't have to be a great artist to sketch something you see.

❁ **Sketch the map of the adventure that day.**

❁ **Personalize it.** Did someone say something funny? What was the most unique thing that happened on the adventure?

❁ **Use it like a scrapbook.** Add any trail brochure or ticket to your journal to remember your adventure.

A great trail is a story—it has a beginning, a true climax or crux, then an end, whether that's back the way you came or finishing a loop. As you review your outings with young adventurers, encourage them to feel the story of the trail. How did they like the beginning? What was the climax? How did it end? What characters (plants, rock formations, animals) stood out to them? A fun after-hike activity is taking your nature journal and writing a fictional account of what happened on the trail, making the landscape come alive in a whole new way.

Consider picking out a small blank journal for kids to bring along in their adventure bags. When you stop for lunch at your destination, at power-up stops, on the ride home, or later that night, encourage your little adventurers to create drawings of things they saw, document their observations of trees or animals, or press leaves they found on the ground.

DIGITAL CONNECTIONS

The social media accounts of many of the agencies that manage park lands in Illinois, Indiana, and Ohio are quite active, and they can be a great way for kids to use technology to enhance their experience in nature. They can ask pre- or post-adventure questions about conditions or flora and fauna, and the forums can be wonderful vehicles for sharing images you snapped—for both you and your little adventurer. Search the location on Instagram for recent photos, and be sure to geo-tag yours to contribute to other hikers' searches as well. Enhance the journey and encourage them to define what really stood out to them about the experience with a coauthored trip report on one of these sites:

 AllTrails.com This is a crowd-sourced database of hikes built by a community of 4 million registered members that includes reviews, user-uploaded photos, and downloadable maps. Meaghan Praznik, head of communications at AllTrails, says, "We all know why the outdoors are important. Health benefits, physical benefits, and what it does for us mentally. At the end of the day, we want AllTrails to be the how. We want features that will take away stress on how to get outside, because the outdoors should be your escape from the stress. From sorting based on the area you're in, to providing driving directions to the trailhead, to filtering based on criteria suitable for you—whether that's for a new hike you're exploring with three kids or something dog-friendly, we want to make sure we're giving people the confidence to hit the trail."

WeAreOutGrown.org Director of programs, Kayla Klein, describes her organization's appeal like this: "My biggest tip? Take the step! We have a lot of families (me included before I started) who research but don't go. It took me a while, getting over it and getting outside and finding out what this community is all about, like our No Hiker Left Behind philosophy. Everyone is there for the same thing—to get babies and families outside. Go to Communities, find your localized community, and it will have your Facebook group there for your specific city and your city's Ambassadors, where you can find group hikes to go on with other families."

WildflowerSearch.com This site has many good tools for identifying flowers. It's as simple to use as uploading a photo and asking it to scan a database for you. It also has up-to-date lists of species in bloom.

iNaturalist.org and Seek by iNaturalist This web- and app-based online community allows you to share your species observations with other naturalists around the world. It's also a great place to post a question if you can't identify something you found.

Geocaching.com or the Geocaching app Geocaches are treasures hidden by other people with GPS coordinates posted online. If you're heading out on one of the adventures, check the website or app to see if anyone has hidden a treasure along the trail. If they have, you can use your phone to navigate to it, find it, exchange a treasure item or sign the log, and hide it back where you found it. About twelve years ago, Wendy hid one on a trail, and it's been found more than five hundred times!

RunWildMyChild.com Founder Sara McCarty urges, "encourage your kids to try new things, like hiking with you—you never know what they're going to like. The reason kids want to be on screens is because of connection and socialization—get them outside with a friend and they'll be way more likely to stay outside." She shares ways you can connect with other families through new outdoor activities and the #runwildmychild Instagram community.

SMARTPHONES

You may have picked up this book to find ways of distracting kids from their phones. Not using a phone at all during your adventures can be fun and appropriate—and you probably already know where you stand on the issue of screen time—but if you want to try a balance, letting kids use their phone on the trail to take a picture of an interesting flower, navigate with a digital compass app, use the audio app to capture a birdsong, or share their pictures of the hike on the state

Use apps to identify items along the trail

forest's Instagram can be a conscientious way to bridge technology and outdoor time (just be sure the phone is put away more than it's out).

SHOWING RESPECT FOR NATURE

There are 31 million lovely people living in Illinois, Indiana, and Ohio, and enjoying and protecting our land will be key to conserving its beauty for generations to come. We hope to inspire stewards—the more we are out there understanding and delighting in the natural world with our families, the more we and our little adventurers want to take care of it in the future. Some of the beautiful areas in this guide are also the most remote and precious. You're doing the most important thing you can to keep the states beautiful—taking your kids outside.

When you get to the top of a lookout tower or squeeze through rock ledges with your kids, you can't help but feel a part of something larger.

By simply noticing and beginning to identify features, flora, and fauna in nature, you're creating a sense of respect and appreciation. Model and embrace the "Leave No Trace" ethos (see LNT.org for more great ideas) on each and every trail. Be diligent with snack wrappers and the flotsam and jetsam of your adventure bag. Be sure to always stay on the trail and avoid trampling vegetation and disturbing wildlife to ensure that everyone and everything can share the adventure.

The scavenger hunts will be asking kids to act as young naturalists, to notice, touch, and play with nature around them in a safe and gentle way. For the most part, try not to take a leaf or flower off a growing plant, but rather collect and play with items that are already on the ground. Manipulate them, stack them, create art with them, trace them in journals—but then leave them to be used by other creatures in the area, from the fungi decomposing a leaf to another kid walking down the trail tomorrow. Invite your kids to see if they can help with community science by reporting observations back to ranger stations, cleaning up trash, and volunteering to maintain trails. Many of these wilderness areas and public lands were created with the help of state leaders, and you're creating the next generation of conservationists simply by getting kids out in them.

Conservation is also easier than ever before. Sharon and her kids help scientists studying wildlife that live in and around Chicago through an online program called Chicago Wildlife Watch (chicagowildlifewatch.org). Developed by Lincoln Park Zoo and the Adler Planetarium, it encourages everyone to help researchers understand how animals, from coyotes to chipmunks, share the Chicago ecosystem. Each state's Department of Natural Resources has a web page dedicated to community science programs, from reporting sightings of frogs, butterflies, birds, and bees to turtles and more. Invite your kids to see if they can help with community science by reporting observations back to ranger stations, cleaning up trash, and volunteering to maintain trails.

ADVENTURES IN
ILLINOIS

Adventurers, let's begin in the Prairie State. Founded in 1808, it's the largest state in this guide covering 57,915 square miles. Those miles include diverse habitats, from wetlands to prairies to gorges and hardwood forests. Begin up north, on the shore of Lake Michigan, where the landscape is dominated by marshes, sloughs, fens, and other wetlands created by ancient glaciers. Historically, more than 60 percent of Illinois was prairie, home to 850 indigenous plant species that were referred to as a "sea of grass." Today, the landscape is dominated by agriculture, and less than 1 percent of prairie habitat remains. Traveling south, you'll find a dramatically different landscape at Starved Rock and Matthiessen State Parks—sandstone canyons created by glacial flood waters 16,000 years ago. Make your way south along the Illinois River to explore natural arches, waterfalls, breathtaking bluffs, overlooks, and bald cypress swamps in Shawnee National Forest. Get your adventure bag and power up before setting off on your adventure in the Land of Lincoln!

1

DUNE WALK AT ILLINOIS BEACH STATE PARK

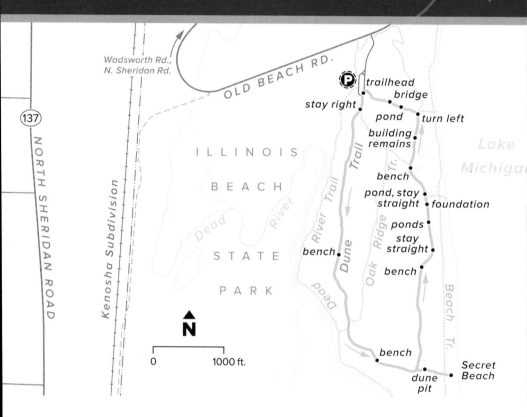

Wadsworth Rd.,
N. Sheridan Rd.

OLD BEACH RD.

137

NORTH SHERIDAN ROAD

Kenosha Subdivision

ILLINOIS

BEACH

STATE

PARK

Dead

River

Dead

River Trail

Dune

Oak Ridge

Dune Trail

Beach Tr.

Lake
Michigan

trailhead
bridge
stay right
pond
turn left
building
remains
bench
pond, stay
straight • foundation
ponds •
stay
straight •
bench •
bench •
bench •
dune • Secret
pit Beach

▲
N

0   1000 ft.

YOUR ADVENTURE

Adventurers, today we'll hike a portion of the 6.5-mile shoreline at Illinois Beach on the historical homeland of the Peoria. Begin counterclockwise and walk through a savannah of black oaks. Listen and look carefully, as there are many birds in the park and over 650 species of plants in the dune area. Stay straight on the Dune Trail and walk until you come to a bench—power

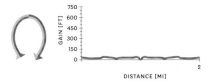

GAIN [FT]
750
600
450
300
150
0

DISTANCE [MI]

LENGTH 2-mile loop

ELEVATION GAIN 20 feet

HIKE TIME + EXPLORE 1.5 hours

DIFFICULTY Easy—short and flat, but fully exposed in summer heat

SEASON Year-round; summer is a great time to cool off by the lakeshore.

GET THERE From Chicago, take US-41 to turn right on Buckley Road / IL-137. Follow north for about 10.5 miles, then take a right onto W Wadsworth Road and follow for 0.5 miles. Continue straight onto Illinois Beach State Park Road and follow as it becomes Old Beach Road. Turn right at the sign for the nature center and the parking lot will be on your right. There are two trailheads—take the farther one to make this a counterclockwise loop.

Google Maps: bit.ly/timberillinoisbeach

RESTROOM At parking lot

FEE None

TREAT YOURSELF Shirl's Drive-In offers burgers, ice cream, and Scooter pies—give it a try! Take Wadsworth Road for 2 miles, then head south 2.6 miles on Lewis Road. The drive-in is on the right.

Illinois Beach State Park
(847) 662-4811
Facebook @IllinoisBeachStatePark

up here. When you reach a second junction with the Oak Ridge Trail, stay straight. Pass another bench and reach a junction—take this short side trail to a secret beach! Play with the fine sand and search for agates in the pebbly shore, then head back to the junction and take a right to close the loop. Can you tell the difference between this part of the trail and the oak savannah? What is different? Pass another bench, stay straight past a side trail, and reach seasonal ponds and the remains of an old building. Pass one more pond and bench, staying straight, until you reach a sign—that's your cue to turn left back to the parking lot. Cross a cool bridge, stopping for a moment to look for wildlife in the marsh below, before wrapping up. Make a weekend of it and camp at the Illinois Beach State Park Campground.

SCAVENGER HUNT

Black oak

Welcome to the savannah, a grassy plain with a few trees. Look around—how is this land different than a forest or the beach ecosystem? Plopped here and there are these deciduous (loses its leaves) trees with their darker black bark. Find one of the leaves and count how many lobes it has and touch the bristles on the end.

Quercus velutina (means "velvety" in Latin, for the soft underside of its leaves)

Green frog

You may spot this amphibian hopping from the savannah to the ocean. They breathe through their lungs on land like us, but underwater they breathe through their skin, which carries oxygen to the rest of the body. Would you rather live on land, water, or both like the frog?

Rana clamitans

Jewelweed

Look for big ovate (round like an egg) leaves with soft teeth on the edge. During summer and fall, this plant has a bright orange flower with red spots. Water beads on them like little jewels. They're also called touch-me-nots. In fall, you might notice their seedpods hanging. If you softly touch them, it triggers a spring inside to burst open and spread the seeds. Pretend to be a seedpod and let a friend touch your head to make you pop.

Impatiens capensis in full bloom

Rockhounding

The shore of Lake Michigan tumbles a variety of rocks and even special agates (polished gems that have banded layers). How many different colors can you find? How many different textures?

Rough vs. smooth

Lake Michigan

Be sure to stop, power up, and watch the waves lap the shoreline of the third largest lake in the country. It's 22,406 square miles. How long do you think it would take you to swim across it? You're on a special kind of beach called a beach-ridge plain, with mounds of sand that have been built up by waves.

Take a deep breath and enjoy the lakeshore

2

LINGER ON LEATHERLEAF BOG AT MORAINE HILLS STATE PARK

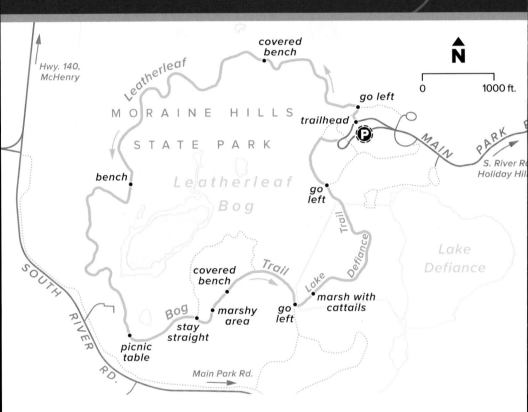

On the map:

Hwy. 140, McHenry

covered bench

N

0   1000 ft.

Leatherleaf

go left

trailhead

MORAINE HILLS

STATE PARK

MAIN

PARK

S. River Rd.
Holiday Hil

bench

Leatherleaf

Bog

go left

Trail

Lake
Defiance

Lake Defiance

covered bench

Trail

go left

marsh with cattails

Bog

marshy area

go left

stay straight

picnic table

SOUTH RIVER RD.

Main Park Rd.

YOUR ADVENTURE

Adventurers, today you'll explore prairies, marshes, and meadows surrounding Leatherleaf Bog. People have been living on this land seasonally as far back as 6000 years ago. The Native American Peoria tribe lived here before European settlement. You'll follow the blue loop, called the Leatherleaf Bog Trail. Start out by going right at the trailhead. The wide, crushed

Enjoy a variety of habitats along this trail →

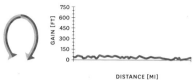

GAIN [FT]

750
600
450
300
150
0

DISTANCE [MI]

LENGTH 3.2-mile loop

ELEVATION GAIN 105 feet

HIKE TIME + EXPLORE 2 hours

DIFFICULTY Moderate—flat, but longer hike along a wide trail

SEASON Year-round, but fall is an ideal time for temperature, changing colors, and seeing migrating sandhill cranes that stop over on their way south. This path can be used for snowshoeing or cross-country skiing in winter.

GET THERE Take US-12 west to the IL-176 W / W Liberty Street exit in Wauconda. Follow 3.4 miles, then take a slight right onto S. River Road. At the traffic circle, continue straight on River Road for 1.4 miles. Turn right into Moraine Hills State Park on Main Park Road (it will become Comes Trail) to reach the parking lot and trailhead.

Google Maps: bit.ly/timbermorainehills

RESTROOM At trailhead

FEE None

TREAT YOURSELF Get shaved ice at My Flavor It!, located on Main Street in Wauconda about 8 miles from the park.

Moraine Hills State Park
(815) 385-1624
Facebook @MoraineHillsStatePark

gravel path meanders through shaded woods and by open prairies, providing varieties of habitats for a diversity of plants and animals. This area is particularly noteworthy for bird-watching. As you walk, listen to the sounds. You may find evidence along the trail of some of the park's mammal residents like deer, raccoons, foxes, and coyotes. There are numerous benches along the trail to rest and observe nature. About halfway around the loop, come to an educational panel about Leatherleaf Bog. Bogs are like marshes but with spongy, acidic ground. Look for the evergreen shrub that gives this bog its name. Leatherleaf is a threatened species in Illinois and protected within this park. Next you'll reach a picnic table near an unmarked offshoot trail. Keep left and stay on the main path. Pass Fox Hollow Nature Path on your left, which loops and reconnects to this main trail. Continue straight until you reach a creek and then a junction with the Lake Defiance Trail. Turn left, following the blue blaze to remain on the Leatherleaf Bog Trail. Pass a marsh filled with cattails on the right, with Lake Defiance in the distance. Stay left at a final junction before ending back at the trailhead.

SCAVENGER HUNT

Coyotes

These mammals are an important part of this ecosystem. They look like small wolves or large dogs. They can be shy, so you may not see one, but you might find evidence of them, like scat along the trail or tracks in the dirt or snow.
Coyotes are very vocal, with long howls and sharp yips and barks. See if you can imitate a coyote howling, yipping, and barking.

Canis latrans leaves scat (poop) on the trail

Seasonal special: sandhill cranes

These large birds are gray with a patch of red on their head. They have wingspans of 5 to 7 feet. From mid-September through November each year, thousands of them migrate south for winter, stopping over in Illinois. The marshes of Moraine Hills are a favorite place

for them to rest and eat on their journey. Spread your arms wide. Do you think your arm span is longer or shorter than a crane's wingspan?

Antigone canadensis

Smooth sumac

This native shrub is particularly beautiful in fall, when its leaves turn bright orange and red and it develops large red berry clusters that many animals love to eat. Feel the stem of the plant. Does it feel smooth or hairy? If it feels smooth, it's a smooth sumac. If it feels hairy, it is likely a staghorn sumac, a close relative that looks similar.

Rhus glabra

Cattails

This perennial (comes back every year) grass may look like a corndog, but it doesn't taste like one. It is, however, a favorite food for Canada geese and some rodents. Cattails also provide shelter for fish, frogs, and snakes, as well as nesting materials for numerous species. Gently touch the brown cone (the female flower). What does it feel like?

Typha latifolia (means "broad-leafed" in Latin, for its long, flat leaves)

3

CIRCLE RIVERBEND TRAIL IN THE FULLERSBERG WOODS

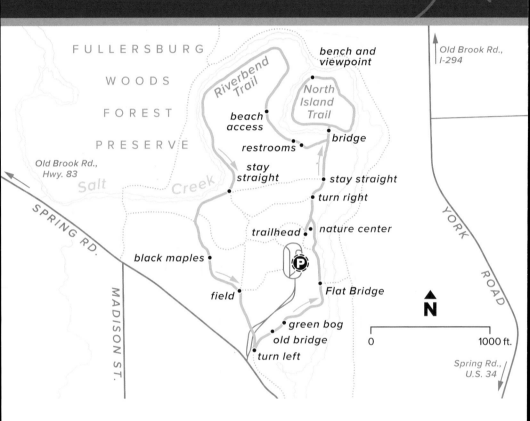

FULLERSBURG

WOODS

FOREST

PRESERVE

Riverbend Trail

beach access

restrooms

stay straight

Old Brook Rd., Hwy. 83

Salt

Creek

bench and viewpoint

North Island Trail

bridge

stay straight

turn right

nature center

trailhead

Old Brook Rd., I-294

YORK ROAD

SPRING RD.

MADISON ST.

black maples

field

green bog

old bridge

turn left

Flat Bridge

N

0   1000 ft.

Spring Rd., U.S. 34

YOUR ADVENTURE

Adventurers, today you're on the historical homeland of the Peoria. You'll be following 43.4-mile-long Salt Creek, a tributary of the 133-mile Des Plaines River, which feeds into the 237-mile Illinois River, and eventually the 2,320-mile-long Mississippi River! It was named because in the nineteenth century, a wagonload of salt was accidentally spilled in it. Oops.

Huge trees provide a canopy over you the entire hike →

GAIN [FT]

750
600
450
300
150
0

2.6

DISTANCE [MI]

LENGTH 2.6-mile lollipop loop

ELEVATION GAIN 52 feet

HIKE TIME + EXPLORE 1.5 hours

DIFFICULTY Easy, short, mostly flat, wide gravel trail

SEASON Year-round; spring and fall are perfect for bird-watching (and flowers and foliage, respectively)

GET THERE Take US-34 W / E Ogden Avenue and turn north on York Road for 0.2 miles. Turn left onto Spring Road for 0.5 miles, then turn right into the nature center parking area.

GOOGLE MAPS: bit.ly/timberfullersburg

RESTROOM At trailhead

FEE None

TREAT YOURSELF Get five ice cream flavors stacked high at Original Rainbow Cone—just 14 minutes west on Roosevelt Road in Lombard.

Forest Preserve District of DuPage County
(630) 850-8110
Facebook @fullersburgwoods

From the nature center, head counterclockwise on the blue Riverbend Trail, which you'll follow signs for the whole way. Stay right and then right again past the Oriole Trail, and power up on a bench if you need it. Cross the North Island bridge and head around the island clockwise, resting at one of several shelters if needed. Be sure to stop off at creek access points to look for critters like frogs. After crossing the bridge again, keep going along the Riverbend Trail. Pass two restrooms and another shelter, and continue to follow Salt Creek. Stay straight past the Oriole trail again, and relax at the Adirondack Chair Chill Shelter. Pass the Monarch Trail to continue on the blue Riverbend Trail. Walk past a big stand of black maples on your left, and pass a huge field with picnic shelters until you carefully cross the road. Turn left after the road, back on the Riverbend Trail, passing Flat Bridge back to the nature center where you started.

SCAVENGER HUNT

Black raspberries
Look for the brambles of this plant protecting its berries—their leaves have serrated (jagged) edges. In spring you might find white flowers blooming on the vines.

Rubus occidentalis

Eastern cottonwood
Look for the fluffy white cotton blowing off of this deciduous (loses its leaves) tree's branches in spring. Female trees grow seed pods which burst open and release the cotton (its seeds) to help it reproduce. Catch a piece of cotton as it "snows" on top of you! The leaves turn a brilliant yellow in fall.

Populus deltoides (means "triangle" in Latin, for its triangle-shaped leaves)

Eastern black walnut

Fan yourselves with this deciduous (loses its leaves) tree's long pinnate leaves (smaller leaflets on opposite sides of one another) in summer. You might find something different hanging off of it each season. Look for the thick green hulls (the covering of the nuts) in summer, and when they drop, look for the walnuts or the empty hulls from animals snacking on the nuts. What's your favorite nut?

Juglans nigra

Ohio buckeye

In summer, you'll find these spiky nut-like seeds hanging from the limbs above you and falling on the ground—they're buckeyes! Inside the spiky husk is the actual seed. It's black with a dot in the middle that looks a bit like a deer's eye. Collect as many husks or seeds that you can find on the ground and arrange them in a pattern. Let a hiking partner look at it for 30 seconds, then mess it up and see how good their memory is to put the pattern back together! Then return them to where you found them.

Aesculus glabra (means "hairless" in Latin, for its smooth leaves)

Northern leopard frog

These amphibians have a cool leopard-like spotting on their backs. You might find them crossing the road to get to the pond. Watch them jump with their long, powerful legs, and then have a "frog-race" with your hike mates. Who won?

Rana pipiens

4

OGLE OAKS AT LITTLE RED SCHOOLHOUSE NATURE CENTER

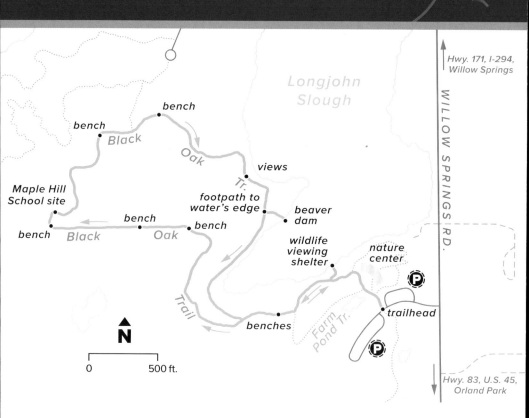

YOUR ADVENTURE

Adventurers, today you journey back through time at the Little Red School-house Nature Center. Inside, learn about the Potawatomi who once lived in this area, with an example of a wigwam. Then start on the Farm Pond Trail directly behind the Little Red Schoolhouse to the left. First, turn to the right and check out the lookout over Longjohn Slough (pronounced "sloo";

Many children learned reading, writing, and arithmetic here over 100 years ago →

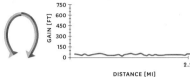

GAIN [FT]

750
600
450
300
150
0

2.2

DISTANCE [MI]

LENGTH 2.2-mile loop

ELEVATION GAIN 64 feet

HIKE TIME + EXPLORE 1.5 hours

DIFFICULTY Easy—short and flat crushed stone path

SEASON Year-round; summer is a lovely time to view osprey, hummingbirds, and bird migrations. Bug spray is helpful in summer; fall offers wonderful colors as the trees change.

GET THERE From Chicago, take I-294 to Exit 22 toward Willow Springs Road. Turn right on 75th Street and go half a mile, then turn left on Willow Springs Road for 3.3 miles. Enter the Little Red Schoolhouse Nature Center on your right.

Google Maps: bit.ly/timberlittleredschoolhouse

RESTROOM At nature center

FEE None

TREAT YOURSELF Kirschbaum's Bakery in nearby Western Springs, about 8 miles north of the trailhead, has been a family-owned bakery for over sixty years. Take-out only, they offer cookies, pastries, cakes, and more—perfect for your adventure bag.

Little Red Schoolhouse Nature Center
(708) 839-6897 | Facebook
@LittleRedSchoolhouseNatureCenter

it is a swamp/shallow lake), a designated wildlife refuge. Back on the trail you'll pass open prairie—how many different varieties of wildflowers can you spot? You'll then enter the shaded black oak forest. Keep your eyes open for chipmunks, squirrels, and other forest-dwelling creatures. At the fork, go left at the bench and black oak sign (you'll return on the other end). Pass several benches before reaching the original site of the schoolhouse. The trail loops around, passing more benches, and makes its way to the water's edge. Explore the offshoot paths to the water. At the end of one you may find a beaver lodge. What animals can you spot? When you're done, turn left, pass a nesting box, reconnect left to the Farm Pond Trail, and follow it back to the nature center. Consider staying the weekend and camping nearby at Camp Bullfrog Lake.

SCAVENGER HUNT

Black oak

These large deciduous trees (lose their leaves every year) are all over the path, which explains the trail's name. "*Veluntina*" refers to the underside of the leaves, which are covered with fine hairs. Pick up a leaf. Can you feel the hairs?

Quercus velutina

Great blue heron

Look for this tall, striking bird with a long S-shaped neck and pointed bill. It loves marshes, swamps, ponds, lakes, and flooded fields along the shoreline of rivers. It migrates through the Midwest and is a summer resident before heading south for winter. What do you like to do to stay warm?

Ardea herodias

Swamp roses

This tall, bright perennial (blooms every year) flower has five pink petals. They bloom from early to late summer. The red fruits are called rose hips and have a bunch of seeds inside that birds love to take away and snack on. This spreads seeds so the flower can grow in other places. Sit quietly by the rose and sketch it in your nature journal.

Hibiscus grandiflorus ("big flowers" in Latin)

Lily pads

Can you spot these floating plants? There are thousands of them covering Longjohn Slough in summer. Their stems stretch to roots on the slough bottom. They provide food for animals like muskrats, and many birds love their seeds and stems. The floating leaves provide perches for frogs—can you spot any?

Nymphaea tuberose

Beaver lodge

Keep an eye out for *Caster canadensis*, the largest rodent (mammals with ever-growing teeth for gnawing) in North America, recognizable by their

large flat tail. They build and maintain houses called lodges made from sticks, mud, and rocks. They are so well built that even in winter, the inside of the lodge will not drop below freezing. Can you find a beaver lodge or spot any beaver activity, like chewed trees, along the trail?

Beavers build their home with mud and sticks

5

MEW LIKE A CATBIRD AT MCKEE MARSH

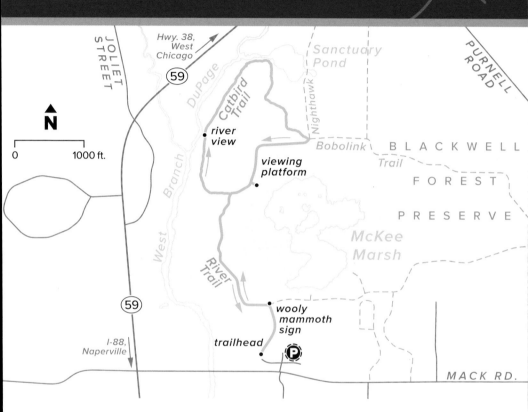

Hwy. 38, West Chicago

59

DuPage

Catbird Trail

N

0   1000 ft.

river view

viewing platform

West Branch

River Trail

59

I-88, Naperville

Sanctuary Pond

Nighthawk

Bobolink Trail

B L A C K W E L L

F O R E S T

P R E S E R V E

McKee Marsh

PURNELL ROAD

wooly mammoth sign

trailhead

P

MACK RD.

YOUR ADVENTURE

Adventurers, today you'll explore the historical homeland of the Peoria, a land shaped by the Wisconsin Glacier 12,000 to 15,000 years ago. It features oak savannahs, marsh, and prairies. The narrow entry trail leads to a wider crushed stone path. An educational panel explains the magnificent 1977 discovery here of a 13,000-year-old woolly mammoth skeleton. You can see

Enjoy prairie, wetland, and forest on this trail →

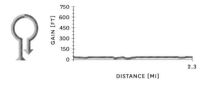

750
600
450
GAIN [FT]
300
150
0
2.3
DISTANCE [MI]

LENGTH 2.3-mile lollipop loop

ELEVATION GAIN 26 feet

HIKE TIME + EXPLORE 1.5 hours

DIFFICULTY Easy—wide, crushed stone path good for strollers

SEASON Year-round. Fall has great colors and migrating birds; spring features wild-flowers; summer features waterfowl and egrets; winter provides few visitors and a chance to spot wildlife and their tracks.

GET THERE From IN-59 in Warrenville, head east on Mack Road and proceed for 1 mile. Turn right into McKee Marsh and park in the lot on the left by the trailhead.

Google Maps: bit.ly/timbermckeemarsh

RESTROOM At trailhead

FEE None

TREAT YOURSELF Pick a cone and some toppings at Kimmer's Premium Homemade Ice Cream in Wheaton, about 6 miles from the trail.

Blackwell Forest Preserve
(630) 933-7200
Facebook @DupageForest

this skeleton on display at the Fullersburg Woods Nature Education Center. Go left on the West Branch Dupage River Trail. Look around at the prairie wildflowers along the trail. You might spot bees, butterflies, birds, and other creatures. Pass a nesting box and come to a trail connection where the terrain changes. Take the mowed-grass and dirt Catbird Trail on the left. Follow this trail through shaded forest toward the West Branch Dupage River. Listen for the mewing of catbirds in the shadowed understory and look for wildlife tracks on the trail. Next, the river comes into view. The path follows it and turns the bend near Sanctuary Pond. Look for frogs and dragonflies, then follow the path back toward McKee Marsh, where it connects with the wide West Branch River Trail. Turn right and reach a viewing platform on the left, overlooking the marsh. You'll likely spot many birds. Follow the path back toward the trailhead. Consider making it a weekend and staying at the nearby Blackwell Family Campground.

SCAVENGER HUNT

Yellow Indiangrass

Walk by this beautiful prairie grass with a golden color. It grows taller than some people. Stand next to it. Who is taller, you or the grass? Look closely at its brown seed head that looks like a feather.

Sorghastrum nutans

American goldfinch

Hold onto your potato chips! If you hear a bird that sounds like it is quietly saying po-ta-to-chip, look around for the brilliant yellow flash of this songbird. Don't worry, it doesn't actually want your potato chips. This bird loves eating only seeds like thistle and sunflower seeds. What do you love eating?

Spinus tristis

Northern leopard frogs

These amphibians face many threats to their survival, but are commonly found here at McKee Marsh. They are named for the irregularly shaped

dark spots on their backs and legs that are reminiscent of leopard spots. Listen for the males' low "snoring" call in spring as they call for their mates. Do you snore when you sleep?

Lithobates pipiens (means "chirping" in Latin)

Gray catbird

Listen for a cat-sounding "mew" while hiking the Catbird Trail. This bird loves the thickets found along part of this trail. Their scientific name, *Dumetella*, means "small thicket," and that is where you will find them. Make a mewing sound and see if they copy you. This bird likes to copy the sounds of other birds.

Dumetella carolinensis

Coneflowers

Coneflowers are some of the many prairie wildflowers you'll find along this trail. The purple coneflower *Echinacea* is prized in traditional medicine. Its scientific name comes from a Greek word that means "sea urchin" or "hedgehog" for its spiky appearance. Give one a very gentle touch. Is it spiky or soft?

Echinacea purpurea

6

CROSS CREEKS AT WHITE PINES FOREST STATE PARK

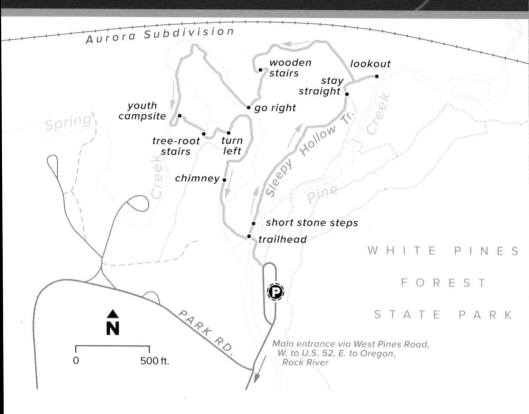

YOUR ADVENTURE

Adventurers, today you'll explore a forest on the historical homeland of the Peoria that is home to a rare stand of virgin white pine. It's one of the only places left in Illinois where they exist. You'll start your adventure with the unique experience of driving through a flowing creek instead of over it on a bridge. Begin by crossing the footbridge to reach the trailhead. The

Cross multiple creeks on this hike →

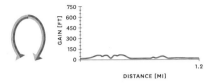

GAIN [FT]

750
600
450
300
150
0

1.2

DISTANCE [MI]

LENGTH 1.2-mile loop

ELEVATION GAIN 118 feet

HIKE TIME + EXPLORE 1.5 hours

DIFFICULTY Challenging—steep elevation in some areas and rugged terrain with tree roots and multiple creek crossings; water hiking shoes recommended

SEASON Spring to fall. Periodic closures for hunting in winter, and the fords to the trailhead are closed from winter to early spring.

GET THERE Take Pines Road west from Oregon and turn left onto S Ridge Road for 0.5 miles, then turn right onto W Pines Road again and go 3.1 miles. Turn right into the park. When you reach the fork, turn left and follow the road over two fords. Park in the lot on the left. The trailhead is on the other side of the footbridge across Pine Creek.

Google Maps: bit.ly/timbersleepyhollowtrail

RESTROOM At trailhead

FEE None

TREAT YOURSELF Grab some gelato or decadent chocolate at Sparklefox Confections, about 8 miles from the park in downtown Oregon.

White Pines Forest State Park
(815) 946-3717
Facebook @IllinoisDNR

orange-blazed Sleepy Hollow trail starts with a steep, short incline up natural stone stairs. Walk along a shaded path of towering pines and come to a left turn—first, go straight to a lookout shelter and bench to power up. Then turn around and head right. Steep stairs will lead you down to Spring Creek, where you'll find fern-covered bluffs and an opportunity to explore around the water. Turn right and follow the creek, then cut back through the woods. You'll cross the creek multiple times as it snakes through the forest. Pass the youth campsite to the right, then carefully climb an incline on tree roots. Take a right to follow the orange blazes, then turn left and pass a massive old walnut tree. Finally, reach the ruin of a stone chimney. Cross the creek again before returning to the trailhead. This park has a historical lodge, cabins, and the Sunny Crest Family Campground nearby. Consider making a weekend of it and exploring other trails too.

SCAVENGER HUNT

Eastern white pine
This conifer (an evergreen tree that doesn't lose its leaves) can easily live two hundred years and could live as long as four hundred! It is the tallest tree in eastern North America. Find a fallen twig and look at its needles. They are bundled

in clusters of five. Find a fallen pine cone. They are narrow and longer than other varieties. Can you make a funny face on the cone using the needles?

Cones and needles of *Pinus strobus*

Tree tumors

Tree burls are tumors that grow on trunks to protect themselves when they get damaged, kind of like a scar you might get on your skin. They are usually round and make a strange bump, or gall, on a tree. This tree has multiple burls. See if you can find a tree with one. Does it feel different or the same as the rest of the bark on the tree? Sketch it in your nature journal.

Burls like the ones on this maple tree are unusual growths

Wood thrush

In summer, listen for the flute-like melody of these songbirds singing in the forest. They like the pine forests, wooded ravines, and creek bluffs in this park. You may hear them before you see them. Try to whistle and imitate a bird call.

Hylocichla mustelina

Stone chimney

Along the trail, you'll see a strange sight— a stone chimney that seems totally out of place. It's all that remains of a small shelter built by the Civilian Conservation Corps in the 1930s. It burned down in the 1970s when somebody built a fire inside the cabin but not in the fireplace. Use your

imagination and tell your trail mates a different, fanciful tale about the history of this chimney. Who lived here? Let your imagination go wild!

A chimney seems out of place in the middle of the forest

7

EXPLORE DELLS CANYON AT MATTHIESSEN STATE PARK

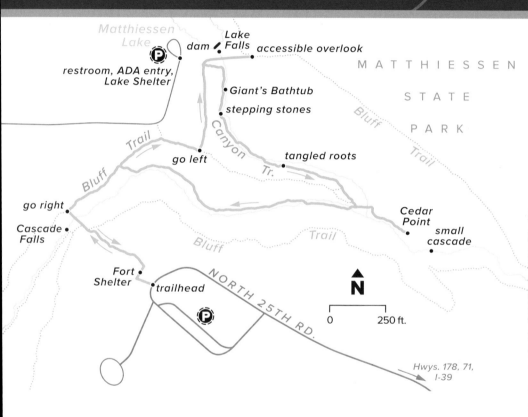

Matthiessen Lake

P

restroom, ADA entry, Lake Shelter

dam / Lake Falls   accessible overlook

M A T T H I E S S E N

S T A T E

P A R K

Giant's Bathtub

stepping stones

Bluff Trail

Canyon Tr.

Trail

Bluff

go left

tangled roots

go right

Cascade Falls

Bluff Trail

Cedar Point

small cascade

Fort Shelter

trailhead

NORTH 25TH RD.

P

▲ **N**

0   250 ft.

Hwys. 178, 71, I-39

YOUR ADVENTURE

Adventurers, today you'll explore unusual rock formations along the Bluff and Dells Canyon trails on the historical homeland of the Peoria and Potawatomi. Begin at the fort and descend stairs to enter Dells Canyon. Cross a bridge and see Cascade Falls. Turn right toward Lower Dells and follow the Bluff Trail along the canyon ridge. Don't descend the first set of

Dells Canyon is an extraordinary landscape →

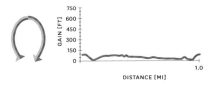

DISTANCE [MI]

LENGTH 1-mile loop

ELEVATION GAIN 200 feet

HIKE TIME + EXPLORE 1.5–2 hours

DIFFICULTY Moderate—steep stairs and rugged terrain along the streambed in the interior of the canyon

SEASON Year-round. Water can be high in spring and fall, making the interior canyon hike more difficult to unpassable in places.

GET THERE From I-80 W, take Exit 81 for IL-178 S. Follow 5.2 miles and turn right on 25th Road, and follow to parking lot. The trailhead is by the fort.

Google Maps: https://bit.ly/timbercanyontrail

RESTROOM At trailhead

FEE None

TREAT YOURSELF Get fudge, chocolates, and ice cream from Roxie's Sweet Confections about 3.5 miles north of the park on IL-178.

Matthiessen State Park
(815) 667-4868
Facebook @StarvedRock

stairs—continue straight. You'll see more stairs down into the canyon—come back to them in a few minutes. First, continue to the bridge and dam overlooking Matthiessen Lake. A parking lot with an accessible trail entrance, Lake Shelter, and restroom will be on your left. On the other side of the bridge is an accessible overlook of Lake Falls. After taking in the views, descend the stairs into the canyon. Head left at the bottom for a view of Lake Falls from beneath. Hike through the canyon—while there aren't many trail markers, you can navigate by following the streambed. The sandstone is colored by minerals seeping through. Ferns, lichen, and moss cling to its cool, moist walls. Stepping stones help you navigate the streambed. Arrive at Giants Bathtub, a body of water covered in duckweed and home to species like frogs, salamanders, and insects. As you follow the streambed, notice the rock formations, unusual trees with tangled roots, and small cascades. The canyon is only about 1 mile long. Just south of Cedar Point is a small waterfall that could be a trickle or a substantial cascade, depending upon the weather. There is a stairway out of the canyon and back up to Bluff Trail here. When the water is high in the canyon, this is a good place to exit because the trail farther ahead can flood. If the water isn't too high, continue following the stream through the dell to the original stairs you passed after the bridge overlooking Cascade Falls. Take them up, turn left, and head back the way you came. Consider making it a weekend and exploring nearby Starved Rock State Park, which offers camping, or check out Cozy Corners Campground nearby.

SCAVENGER HUNT

Cliff swallows

Many birds build nests in trees, but cliff swallows build mud nests in cliff ledges. Can you spot one perching on the canyon walls? Find some mud and sticks and try to build a sturdy nest.

Petrochelidon pyrrhonota (means "flame-colored," like the back of this bird)

Eastern red cedar

The dense evergreen branches of this tree provide shelter for birds, and its blue "berries" (actually cones that house its seeds) are an important food for many species. Smell the bark and branches: does it smell familiar?

Juniperus virginiana

Bullfrog

Look in the water and along the edges. Can you spot, or hear, this amphibian? This large frog gets its name from the sound the male makes, which some people think sounds like the bellowing of a bull. Try to imitate the sound of a bullfrog.

Lithobates (means "stone walker" in Latin) *catesbeianus*

Stepping stones

The stepping stones throughout the canyon make crossing the streambed a fun highlight. Pretend they are lily pads and you're a frog. When you come to these stepping stones, hop across and make ribbit sounds.

Stepping stones

8

STALK WILDCAT CANYON AT STARVED ROCK STATE PARK

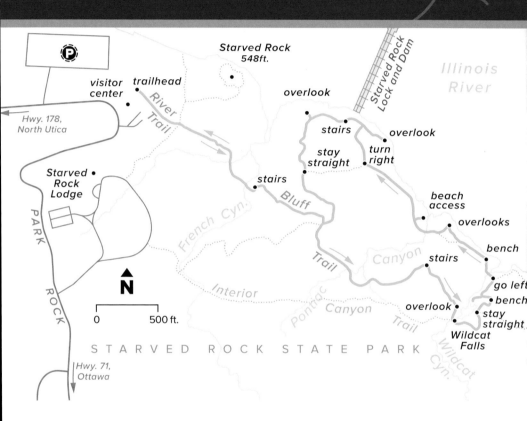

Starved Rock
548ft.

visitor center
trailhead
overlook

Starved Rock
Lock and Dam

Illinois
River

Hwy. 178,
North Utica

River
Trail

stairs

overlook

stay
straight

turn
right

Starved
Rock
Lodge

stairs

beach
access

PARK

French Cyn.

Bluff

overlooks

bench

Canyon

stairs

N

Trail

Interior

go left

ROCK

0   500 ft.

Pontiac

overlook

bench
stay
straight

Canyon

Trail

Wildcat
Falls

STARVED   ROCK   STATE   PARK

Wildcat
Cyn.

Hwy. 71,
Ottawa

YOUR ADVENTURE

Adventurers, today you're climbing some stairs up and down to the bottom of a canyon, to a viewpoint of Starved Rock and more. You're on the historical homeland of the Peoria and Potawatomi. Begin your trek behind the visitor center. You're going to see two of eighteen canyons in this special part of the state, all formed by glacial meltwater and stream erosion. Outside the

The 125-foot-tall Wildcat Falls awaits you →

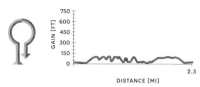

LENGTH 2.3-mile lollipop loop

ELEVATION GAIN 308 feet

HIKE TIME + EXPLORE 2 hours

DIFFICULTY Moderate—up and down on boardwalks but otherwise great, nonrocky terrain

SEASON Year-round; waterfall is strongest in winter and spring, and spring and summer offer spectacular wildflowers

GET THERE From I-80 W, take Exit 81 for IL-178 S. Follow 4.2 miles, turn left on IL-71 E for 1.5 miles, then right on E 950th Road for 0.4 miles. Turn left into the park and park in the lot next to the visitor center; the trail is around the back.

Google Maps: bit.ly/timberstarved

RESTROOM At trailhead

FEE None

TREAT YOURSELF Just five minutes east on the highway is Betty's Pies—a must to bring for a picnic. Feeling adventurous? Try their pie shakes.

Starved Rock State Park
(815) 667-4726
Facebook @StarvedRock

visitor center, you immediately come upon a junction. Stay straight here and follow the signs for French Canyon as you climb the boardwalk stairs. At the top, stay straight for Wildcat Canyon, passing a bench and going up more stairs. Stay left again following signs for Wildcat Canyon. Pass a couple of bridges and look over the top of Pontiac Canyon. Imagine the water rushing over here. Next up is Wildcat Canyon and *two* overlooks. After viewing both, head down the stairs to the bottom of the canyon. Cool off in the shallow pool and see if the flow is rushing or a trickle, depending on the time of year. Power up here and go left on the river trail, turning right for the Beehive Overlook. Keep going and turn right again to climb the stairs for Eagle Cliff and to look out to Starved Rock. Reach another junction and continue right, back on the main trail to return the way you came. Consider camping right there in the park and exploring a different trail the next day.

SCAVENGER HUNT

Seasonal special: mayapple

Look for these huge green umbrella-like leaves and then, in May (hence the name), its beautiful white flower blooms. Each plant has two umbrellas and one flower emerging, which turns into a fruit in summer. If you find a leaf on the ground, trace it in your nature journal.

Podophyllum peltatum

St. Peter Sandstone

425 million years ago, these rocks around you were laid down in an inland sea and later exposed for your enjoyment. Glacial meltwater came through here and carved all the cool canyons in the sandstone around you. What do you think it will look like in another 425 million years?

Sandstone is a sedimentary (deposited in layers over time) rock

Cliff swallow

From the viewpoint deck, keep your eyes peeled for these birds flitting about from the mud nests they build in the cliffs before you. They gather pellets of mud and one by one deposit them to create these cool structures. They live in colonies of hundreds of birds—how many people would you be comfortable living with?

Petrochelidon pyrrhonota (*petros* means "rock" in Greek, and *khelidon* means "swallow")

Leaf galls

These insects munch on the leaves of trees, which releases a toxin that makes the leaf release a hormone to create a little home (gall) for it. This is called a parasitic relationship where one species takes from another without benefiting the host. Can you think of any other parasitic relationships in nature?

Polka dots from gall aphids spot this leaf

Red elderberry

The beautiful burst of red berries on the elder comes from its clusters of flowers, called inflorescences. The berries look like little fireworks exploding with color. Catch the white flowers in spring, and the lance-shaped leaves with tiny teeth from spring to fall. See if you can count how many berries are on just one cluster.

Sambucus racemosa

9

WANDER THE ILLINOIS RIVER BLUFF AT ROBINSON PARK

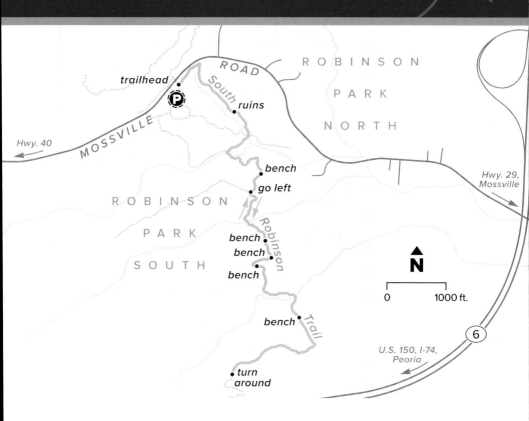

YOUR ADVENTURE

Adventurers, today you'll explore a portion of the Illinois River Bluff Trail through a dedicated nature preserve on the historical homeland of the Peoria. The South Robinson trail begins by crossing several small bridges over multiple creeks in Moon Hollow. Journey on a dirt trail through a deeply shaded forest of oak, sugar maples, and hickory. Look closely to spot

Escape into nature →

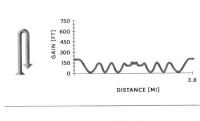

GAIN [FT]

750
600
450
300
150
0

3.8

DISTANCE [MI]

LENGTH 3.8 miles out and back

ELEVATION GAIN 814 feet

HIKE TIME + EXPLORE 2.5–3 hours

DIFFICULTY Challenging—longer, with more elevation gain, but can easily be shortened

SEASON Year-round. Fall is an especially beautiful time to visit, when leaves are changing colors.

GET THERE From IL-29, turn west on Mossville Road and follow for 1.7 miles. The parking lot with the trailhead will be on the left.

Google Maps: bit.ly/timberrobinson

RESTROOM At trailhead (April to mid-October; other times of year, at gas station less than 1 mile west)

FEE None

TREAT YOURSELF Enjoy Sweet CeCe's frozen yogurt, located about 5.5 miles south on N Prospect Road.

Robinson Park
(309) 682-6684
Facebook @PeoriaParkDistrict

old ruins along the trail, about a half mile from the trailhead. They are sure to spark your curiosity and imagination. Just after the ruins, cross a stream over a bridge and come to a larger bridge over a creek. A wayfinder map in Strawberry Hollow helps you see your progress. Cross another bridge and take a steep incline—power up at the top, where there's a bench after the next wayfinder. Soon you'll take a left and see an informational sign about the Illinois Nature Preserve you're hiking in. Cross another two bridges, then pass three benches as you navigate up and down the rolling hills. Pass one final bridge over a creek and a final bench. Before you get to Route 6, reach a wayfinder map that indicates the end of this portion of the trail. Turn around and head back the same way you came.

SCAVENGER HUNT

Ruins

Look closely along the side of the trail and you'll spot a rusted bathtub, water pump, and concrete foundation. These are from an old farmstead that was active here before World War II. Entertain your trail mates with a story. Use your imagination—tell them about the farm and family who lived here.

Mysterious ruins in the forest

Red-headed woodpecker

These birds are unique because they store food in wood cracks and under bark. They eat insects, seeds, and nuts and have a bold black-and-white pattern and strikingly beautiful red head. Look closely at the bark of a nearby tree. Where would you hide your snack?

Melanerpes erythrocephalus (means "red-headed" in Latin)

Chinquapin oak

There are twenty species of oak trees in Illinois, and several of them can be found on this trail. The name *chinquapin* is derived from the Algonquian language, meaning "great berries or fruit." Find a leaf on the ground, then make a rubbing in your nature journal and compare it to other oak species you've found.

Quercus muehlenbergii

Fox

These mammals are mostly active at night, but you may find evidence they have been nearby. Look for scat (their poop) along the trail. Foxes, coyotes, and domestic dogs are all canines. Do you know how to tell the difference between the poop of a pet and a wild canine? Look for hair, berries, or bones in their scat, and twisted ends.

Urocyon cinereoargenteus and scat

Great Goldilocks moss

Believe it or not, you can find Goldilocks in these woods. But not the one from the fairytale. Look for a clumpy, hairy moss commonly called Great

Goldilocks or hair moss. Its scientific name is derived from ancient Greek words *polys*, meaning "many" and *thrix* meaning "hair." *Commune* means community. Can you find the "great hair community?" When you do, find some sticks, stones, or leaves and fashion that hair moss into a wig with a face.

Polytrichum commune

10

DISCOVER MYSTERIOUS CARVINGS AT ROCKY GLEN PARK

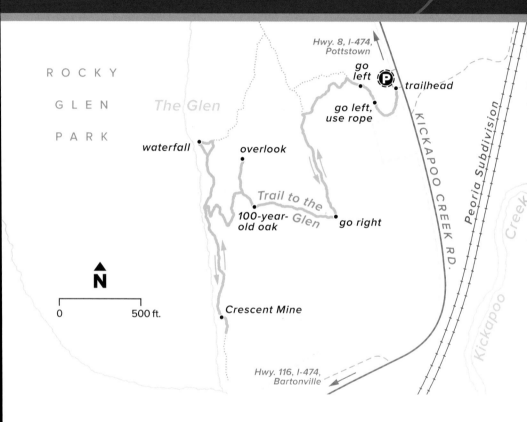

ROCKY

GLEN

PARK

The Glen

Hwy. 8, I-474, Pottstown

go left

trailhead

go left, use rope

waterfall

overlook

Trail to the

100-year-old oak

Glen

go right

N

0   500 ft.

Crescent Mine

KICKAPOO CREEK RD.

Peoria Subdivision

Creek

Kickapoo

Hwy. 116, I-474, Bartonville

YOUR ADVENTURE

Adventurers, today you'll explore a box canyon on the historical homeland of the Potawatomi and Peoria. You'll be searching for hundreds of rock carvings by coal miners. Begin by climbing uphill—this part is challenging. Notice the rope hand-holds along the trail to help you, and be sure to power up as you need it. The trail splits—take the left side, with stairs and a bench

Hike this beautiful valley →

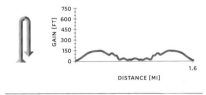

DISTANCE [MI]

LENGTH 1.6-mile out and back

ELEVATION GAIN 348 feet

HIKE TIME + EXPLORE 1.5 hours

DIFFICULTY Moderate—rougher, sometimes steep, muddy, uneven terrain

SEASON Year-round. A small seasonal waterfall is most showy in spring. In winter, the smaller waterfall can freeze from the ground up into a 30-foot stalagmite.

GET THERE From Peoria, head west on IL-116 / W Lincoln Avenue and turn right onto Airport Road for 0.2 miles, then left onto Kickapoo Creek Road for 1 mile. You'll see the small parking area for the trailhead on the left.

Google Maps: bit.ly/timberrockyglen

RESTROOM At gas station about 1 mile southeast of trailhead on Farmington Road

FEE None

TREAT YOURSELF Stop for a creamy cone at Las Delicias Mexican Ice Cream, about 3 miles away on Main Street.

Rocky Glen Park
(309) 682-1200
Facebook @friendsofrockyglen
Facebook @peoriaparkdistrict

along the path. At the plateau, the trail forks at another bench. Go right, following the signs to Rocky Glen. Pass a prairie meadow, take a right, pass another bench, and look for signs to find the one-hundred-year-old oak tree. Reach a junction toward Top of the Glen. Walk to the right to Rocky Glen overlook to see the box canyon and waterfall below. Sadly, you'll also see where people have damaged the environment with graffiti. Power up at the bench here. Head back toward the trail split and turn right, heading down. Pass a bench and descend stairs into the canyon. Signs explain how coal is made and share that this canyon was a secret gathering place for coal miners to rally to form a union. Turn left and walk along the streambed toward Crescent Mine. It is gated off for safety, but it shows what life might have been like for men who worked in dangerous conditions underground. Now head back the way you came. At the stairs, go straight toward the box canyon. Look at the rock face and find hundreds of names and dates etched into the stone, dating as far back as 1880. You'll also see a seasonal waterfall. After spending time here, follow the stream back toward the stairs and climb to the plateau. Go right and follow the trail back to the intersection, then turn right and head back to the trailhead.

SCAVENGER HUNT

Mysterious carvings

Can you find the carving of a hand holding a card? Dave Pittman, president of Friends of Rocky Glen, says, "Consider . . . what these miners endured in such tough working conditions. They worked before dawn until after dark, six days a week. The carved pictures and initials in the rock are something greater than unique art. For people who had nothing, the notion of a union (an organization that helps worker's rights) was the notion of hope for a better future for their children."

Historians think this carving represents a union card

Crescent Mine entrance

Coal is a rock made from ancient plant and animal remains. It is a fossil fuel still extracted today to supply energy, but it creates pollution and contributes to climate change. Digging coal (called extraction) was dangerous work and the mines would sometimes collapse.

The entrance to the coal mine that was operational from 1908–1922

100-year-old oak tree

There aren't many ancient trees in this forest, but one oak tree stands larger than others. Can you find one estimated to be over one hundred years old? Give a tree a hug. Can you get your arms all the way around? If so, it's probably not that old.

Quercus alba

Ebony spleenwort

Mosses, ferns, and lichen flourish in the canyon's cool, moist environment. Look for ebony spleenwort, an evergreen fern with ladderlike dark green oblong leaflets. How are they similar or different than the leaves of other ferns?

Asplenium platyneuron

11

SOAR LIKE AN EAGLE AT PERE MARQUETTE STATE PARK

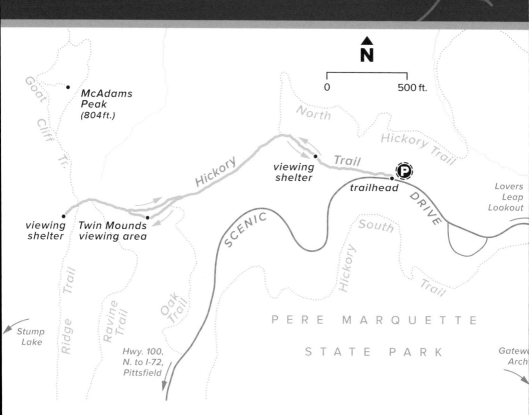

YOUR ADVENTURE

Adventurers, today you will take the short, shady Hickory Trail to an epic overlook in one of Illinois's largest state parks and the historical homeland of the Kaskaskia. Start your experience with a stop at the visitor center, then make your way on the scenic drive to the trailhead with red heart blazes. Not long after beginning your trek, you'll see a shelter on the left

Epic views of the Illinois River and lakes below →

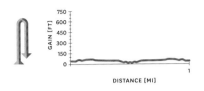

GAIN [FT]

750
600
450
300
150
0

DISTANCE [MI]

1

LENGTH 1-mile out and back

ELEVATION GAIN 82 feet

HIKE TIME + EXPLORE 1 hour

DIFFICULTY Easy—short and flat trail

SEASON Year-round. January and February are exceptional for seeing bald eagles.

GET THERE Take US-67 north from St. Louis to turn left onto W Broadway, which turns into IL-100 N / Great River Road / McAdams Pkwy. Follow it for 20.9 miles. Turn right onto Scenic Drive, entering Pere Marquette State Park. The first small parking area on the left is the trailhead. If you get to Eagle's Roost viewing area, you've gone a bit too far.

Google Maps: bit.ly/timberhickorytrailhead

RESTROOM At lodge and visitor center

FEE None

TREAT YOURSELF Try the warm brown butter cake at the Pere Marquette Lodge.

Pere Marquette State Park
(618) 786-3323
Facebook @PereMarquetteSP

built by the Civilian Conservation Corps in the 1930s—power up here for the rest of your journey. When the trail splits, go left. You'll reach another junction with the Oak Trail—stay right on the Hickory Trail. Soon the trail splits again. Take the left side, staying straight at another connector trail, to reach a river view at Twin Mounds viewing area. Soon the split trail meets again and you'll reach another left turn on the Ravine Trail that goes back to the lodge—stay straight here to reach the McAdams Peak viewing shelter. Enjoy a view of the Illinois River, Swan Lake, Stump Lake, and 12 Mile Island below, and an array of wildlife flying above. Take your time before heading back to the trailhead. Consider staying for the weekend in the historical Pere Marquette Lodge or nearby campgrounds. There are numerous trails to explore in this approximately 9000-acre park.

SCAVENGER HUNT

Long-jawed orb weaver spider

Take a moment to appreciate the art and beauty of this arachnid's spiraling web. These spiders build intricate woven wonders every day to catch insects. The overhang of shelters provides great habitat. Find one of these masterful weavers' webs and draw it in your nature journal.

A member of family Tetragnathidae

Shagbark hickory

This trail is named after these deciduous (loses its leaves) trees, and there are many different kinds. See if you can find a shagbark hickory. An easy giveaway is to look for its shaggy peeling bark. It also drops nuts in fall. If you've ever tasted hickory-flavored food, you can thank this tree. Touch its bark. What does it feel like?

Carya ovata bark

Seasonal special: bald eagle

In January and February, when northern waters freeze over, hundreds of bald eagles come here, where the Mississippi and Illinois rivers meet. This national emblem of the United States has a seven-foot wingspan—spread your arms wide and pretend to soar like an eagle. How big is your "wingspan"?

Haliaeetus leucocephalus (means "white-headed sea eagle" in Latin)

Poison berries

Look but don't poke! The berries of American pokeweed are poisonous to people, but they are an important food for mockingbirds, northern cardinals, and mourning doves who are immune to their toxins. This plant's Latin name, *Phytolacca*, means "red dye plant" because the berries were traditionally used as a natural dye. Can you name another kind of red berry?

Phytolacca americana

American white pelican

This is one of the largest birds in the country. Their wingspan is longer than the tallest human, averaging 8 to 10 feet long. Migratory birds can be spotted here in October and April. Look for a flock of large white birds flying in sync (which means exactly the same way). Pretend you and your trail mates are pelicans. Put your arms out and pretend to fly in sync.

Pelecanus erythrorhynchos (means "red-billed" in Greek)

12

WALK NATURE'S CITY STREETS AT GIANT CITY STATE PARK

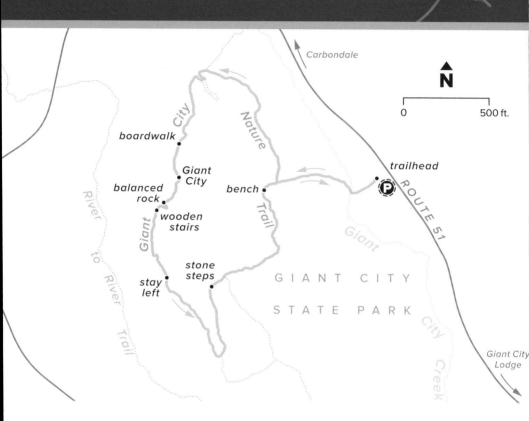

Carbondale

N

0   500 ft.

boardwalk

Giant City

balanced rock

bench

trailhead

wooden stairs

stone steps

stay left

ROUTE 51

GIANT CITY STATE PARK

Giant City Lodge

YOUR ADVENTURE

Adventures, today you'll explore a trail with a famous natural feature that pioneers called a giant city! This park in Southern Illinois, on the historical land of the Miami, is home to lush forests, abundant wildlife, and rock formations like no place else. Humans used its natural wonders for thousands of years, including nomadic Native Americans as far back as 12,000 years.

These geologic formations leave a lasting impression →

750
600
450
300
150
0

GAIN [FT]

DISTANCE [MI]

LENGTH 1-mile lollipop loop

ELEVATION GAIN 190 feet

HIKE TIME + EXPLORE 1 hour

DIFFICULTY Moderate—some elevation, and rugged trail

SEASON Year-round. In spring, waterfalls are rushing; in summer, the bluffs provide natural air-conditioning; in winter, icicles hang from the bluffs and sparkle in the sunlight.

GET THERE Take Walnut Street east out of Carbondale to turn right on Giant City Lodge Road. Follow 9.7 miles, turn right on Church Road, left on Stonefort Road, and bear left onto Giant City Road / US-51. The parking lot will be on your right in about half a mile.

Google Maps: bit.ly/timbergiantcity

RESTROOM At trailhead

FEE None

TREAT YOURSELF Stop at the Giant City Lodge for a variety of cobblers, crisps, or ice cream.

Giant City State Park
(618) 457-4836
Facebook @friendsofgiantcity

The bluffs and shelter caves likely provided protection from weather. Visit the nature center to learn about the unique features and history, then set off on the Nature Trail on an uphill climb. At a fork, turn right and notice a big cave on the left that begs to be explored. Hundreds of years ago, this may have been a great place for a black bear to hibernate, but not today, as bears haven't lived in Illinois since 1822. Follow the trail and you'll come to tall rocks and ledges where moss and ferns cover the walls. Stay left at the next junction and come to a boardwalk next to massive rock ledges. Soon you'll find the famous Giant City, where a sandstone bluff cracked, leaving narrow passageways between enormous sheer-faced stone blocks. Some of these passageways intersect at sharp right angles. They reminded early settlers of city streets and giant buildings. Explore your way through the narrow alleys to come upon Balanced Rock. Take a left to stay on the Nature Trail, then head up some stairs and through the woods until you make your way down-hill. Now turn right, back to the trailhead. There are many trails to explore in this park. Consider making it a weekend and camping at Giant City State Park Campground.

SCAVENGER HUNT

Historical graffiti

Look closely at the "giant city" walls and you may spot carved names and dates from 1862. The Thompson brothers, home from battle during the Civil War, left their permanent mark here. It's now a protected historical artifact because it is one of the only surviving relics of Civil War–era strife between North and South in this region. Today, a good motto to remember when you are in nature is "leave no trace"; don't leave anything behind, including carvings.

Thompson Brothers rock art

Balancing act

Do you dare walk beneath this massive rock that tumbled down a cliff and balanced in this spot? Three hundred million years ago, this was a warm shallow sea. As the waters receded, sand and silt built up into sandstone and made cool rock formations like this one. Play a game with your trail mates. Stand on one foot and see who can stay balanced the longest.

Balanced rock

Coral hedgehog

From August to October look for this bright white fungus. Some people think it looks like coral; others think it resembles teeth. In fact, it has several names, including coral hedgehog and comb tooth fungi. What do you think it looks like?

Hericium coralloides (means "hedgehog" and "coral" in Latin)

Littleflower alumroot

Most flowers like sunshine. Not so for this shade lover. This special plant can only grow in deeply shaded places where direct sun will never reach it. Where on this trail do you think you might find it? Do you know any other species of plants or animals that avoid the sun?

Heuchera parviflora (means "small flower" in Latin)

SWOOP AROUND CACHE RIVER STATE NATURAL AREA

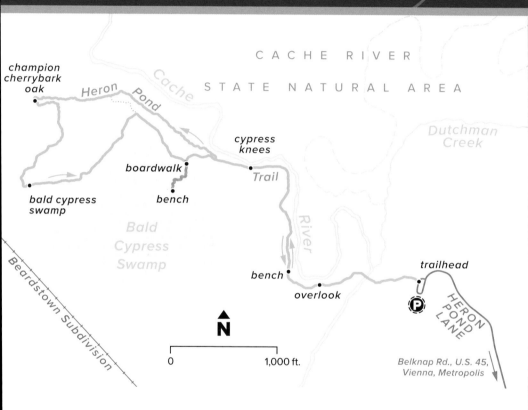

champion cherrybark oak

Heron Pond

Cache

CACHE RIVER STATE NATURAL AREA

Dutchman Creek

cypress knees

boardwalk

Trail

bald cypress swamp

bench

Bald Cypress Swamp

River

Beardstown Subdivision

bench

trailhead

overlook

P

HERON POND LANE

N

0   1,000 ft.

Belknap Rd., U.S. 45, Vienna, Metropolis

YOUR ADVENTURE

Adventurers, today you'll explore an other-worldly wetland unlike anywhere else in the Prairie State. This historical homeland of the Kaskaskia is a remarkable bald cypress and tupelo swamp and is home to over one hundred endangered and threatened plant and animal species. To start, cross a bridge over the Cache River and continue through shaded forest.

This remarkable bald cypress swamp is unlike anywhere else in Illinois →

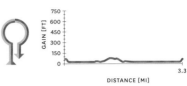

LENGTH 3.3-mile lollipop loop

ELEVATION GAIN 85 feet

HIKE TIME + EXPLORE 1.5–2 hours

DIFFICULTY Moderate—longer hike; for shorter 1.5-mile trip, take Heron Pond trail to boardwalk and back

SEASON Year-round; trail can temporarily close if rain raises the river level.

GET THERE Head south on US-45 to turn right on Belknap Road. In 1.5 miles, go right on Heron Pond Lane following signs for Heron Pond and Little Black Slough Nature Preserve.

Google Maps: bit.ly/timberheronpond

RESTROOM At trailhead

FEE None

TREAT YOURSELF Ned's Shed is about 5 miles away in Vienna. It offers cheese curds, cheesy fries, burgers, and snacks.

Cache River State Natural Area
(618) 657-2064
Facebook @IllinoisDNR
Facebook @FriendsoftheCacheRiverWatershed

Pass a river overlook and cross stepping stones on the creek. At the fork, follow the trail slightly right toward the gigantic state champion cherrybark oak tree. Being a champion means it's the largest specimen of its kind in the entire state! From there, turn around and take the grassy path on the right toward Heron Pond. Follow it to the floating boardwalk to visit the forested depths of the wetland. Imagine you've stepped back in time. This wetland forest has remained relatively untouched for thousands of years. Listen carefully: can you hear the bird-voiced treefrogs singing? Examine the duckweed on the water's surface: can you spot turtles and tiny frogs peeking out? Look up: this is a hotspot for birds, including woodpeckers, songbirds, raptors, and herons. At the end of the boardwalk, retrace your steps and turn right, following the trail back to the fork. Then turn right again and take the path back to the trailhead. Consider staying the weekend and camping nearby at the Shawnee Forest Campground.

SCAVENGER HUNT

Eastern box turtle

Examine the edges of the trail carefully and you might spot a box turtle. They camouflage incredibly well with dried leaves and mud and don't move very fast. If you find one, draw the patterns of its shell in your nature journal.

Terrapene carolina

Bald cypress

This deciduous (loses its leaves every year) conifer (tree with cones) is the only tree with knees! The cone-shaped knees can grow six feet tall and are part of the root system that helps keep the tree standing in unstable wet soils. How many knees can you count?

Taxodium distichum

Pileated woodpecker

All seven woodpecker species found in Illinois are found here. Can you hear them knocking on tree trunks? The pileated woodpecker is the largest species. They make big oval-shaped holes. Look for holes they leave behind—can you find any?

Dryocopus pileatus left these holes

Green frog

Heron Pond is home to between 40–50 species of reptiles and amphibians. Listen carefully. Can you hear the male green frog's call like a banjo string, the chorus and bird-voiced tree-frogs singing, or the deep throaty croaking of bullfrogs? See if you can imitate their sounds.

Lithobates clamitans in Lemnoideae

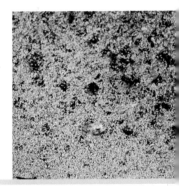

Prothonotary warbler

These small, bright yellow warblers nest in cavities in tree trunks or large branches and breed in forested wetlands. Biologists have been studying them for years. People donate milk and juice cartons to make their nest boxes. How many of these can you spot? Try this craft at home to see if you can attract birds to your nest box.

Protonotaria citrea and a nest box made from a milk carton

14

TRAVERSE A NATURAL BRIDGE AT BELL SMITH SPRINGS

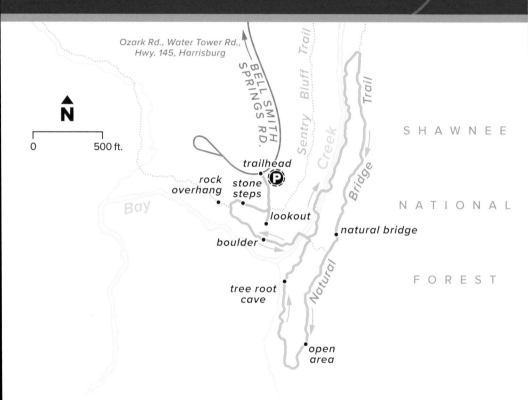

Ozark Rd., Water Tower Rd., Hwy. 145, Harrisburg

N

0   500 ft.

BELL SMITH SPRINGS RD.

Sentry Bluff Trail

Creek Trail

trailhead

rock overhang

stone steps

Bay

lookout

boulder

natural bridge

Bridge

tree root cave

Natural

open area

S H A W N E E

N A T I O N A L

F O R E S T

YOUR ADVENTURE

Adventurers, welcome to one of the most beautiful areas in Shawnee National Forest, on the historical homeland of the Miami. This forest is a national landmark with specialized habitats for over seven hundred species of flowering plants, ferns, and lichens. You'll explore clear, rocky streams, canyons with high sandstone bluffs, and the largest natural bridge in Illinois.

Clear rocky springs, canyons, and wildflowers abound →

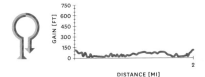

DISTANCE [MI]

LENGTH 2-mile lollipop loop

ELEVATION GAIN 256 feet

HIKE TIME + EXPLORE 2 hours

DIFFICULTY Moderate—steep climb down and back up; creek crossing can be ankle- to calf-deep at times

SEASON Year-round. Spring is a favorite for wildflowers.

GET THERE From Harrisburg, take IN-145 south to Burden Falls Road. Turn right and follow it for 5 miles, then go right onto Ozark Road for 1.4 miles, left on Bell Smith Springs Road and follow to the parking lot.

Google Maps: bit.ly/timberbellsmith

RESTROOM At trailhead

FEE None

TREAT YOURSELF As you head back, have some Southern-style cooking at Murphy's Pit BBQ, about 8 miles northwest from the trailhead.

Shawnee National Forest
(618) 658-2111
Facebook @shawneenatlforest

Descend into the sandstone canyon on the yellow-blazed Natural Bridge Trail on steep stone stairs hand-laid by the Civilian Conservation Corps in the 1930s. Go right at the first junction, and feel the temperature get cooler as you go into the canyon. Come down more stone stairs and reach another junction—turn left toward the yellow Natural Bridge Trail. Pass a cool boulder and use rocks to cross Bay Creek. Can you spot any animals in the water? After crossing the creek, go left, following the yellow blazes. Reach another junction with the blue trail. Stay right to continue on the Natural Bridge trail. When you reach the natural bridge, be careful—the edges are steep! Take in the enormity of the natural stone arch as you walk on it. Once across, the trail leads to an open area with pine trees. Follow the yellow blaze and continue back to the creek crossing. From there, follow the trail back to the parking lot. Consider camping at one of the nearby campgrounds, such as Redbud Campground or Oak Point Campground.

SCAVENGER HUNT

Seasonal special: crayfish/crawdads

Look closely in the shallow water of the creek from spring to October to find these crustaceans (animals with tough outer shells) hiding among the rocks. Four species are endangered and protected. What other animals do you think they resemble?

Twenty-three different species of *Cambarus* live in Illinois

Seasonal special: calico paint caterpillars

Look for these moth larvae from July to October. You may spot them feeding on goldenrod and aster plants during the day. Believe it or not, these colorful critters turn into a dull moth called the brown-hooded owlet. Draw this beauty in your nature journal.

Cucullia convexipennis

Natural bridge

Keep an eye out and watch your step—you might start crossing this massive land bridge before you realize you've arrived. There are sheer drops on both sides, so walk carefully. The bridge is 125 feet high, and the arch is 30 feet wide. It was created along the canyon when several fractures in the sandstone intersected to weaken the rock. Water flowing through the fractures caused the rock wall to collapse, leaving the arch above and a jumble of boulders below.

The tallest natural bridge in Illinois

Reindeer moss

This coral-looking species is actually not a moss at all. It's a lichen, which is formed by fungi and algae. This variety is rare in Illinois. It's commonly called reindeer lichen or rein-deer moss because it's found in the Arctic tun-dra and is a favorite food for reindeer. Gently touch it—what does it feel like? Sketch a rein-deer munching on it in your nature journal.

No reindeer here, just their favorite food, *Cladonia*

Chicken of the woods

This bright orange bracket polypore (means it has pores/tubes on its underside. Get down low—can you see them?) can be found from spring through fall. It's called chicken of the woods because some people suggest its texture is like cooked chicken. Gently touch it. What does it feel like?

Laetiporus (means "bright pores" in Latin)

15

INDULGE IN VIEWS AT GARDEN OF THE GODS

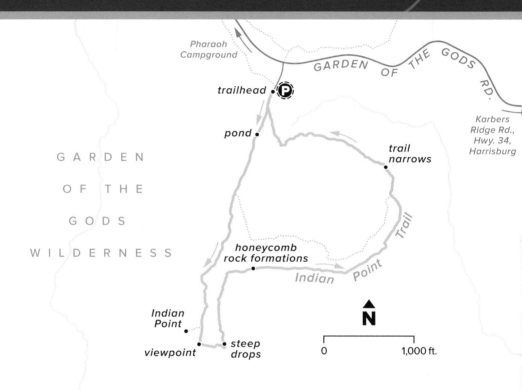

Pharaoh
Campground

GARDEN OF THE GODS RD.

trailhead **P**

Karbers
Ridge Rd.,
Hwy. 34,
Harrisburg

pond •

trail
narrows

G A R D E N

O F T H E

G O D S

W I L D E R N E S S

honeycomb
rock formations

Indian Point Trail

Indian
Point

viewpoint

• steep
drops

N

0   1,000 ft.

YOUR ADVENTURE

Adventurers, today you're going to feel like mountaineers as you take in extraordinary views from the high vista overlooking the rolling Shawnee hills. You'll also explore caves along this terrific trail on the historical homeland of the Miami. As you begin your hike on the Indian Point Trail through the shaded forest, stay right at the first fork to encounter a small

The views from the Indian Point Trail are breathtaking →

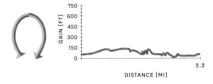

GAIN [FT]

750
600
450
300
150
0

DISTANCE [MI]

2.2

LENGTH 2.2-mile loop

ELEVATION GAIN 223 feet

HIKE TIME + EXPLORE 1.5 hours

DIFFICULTY Moderate—some loose rocks and tree roots, and steep cliffs

SEASON Year-round. Fall offers exceptional views of tree colors at the overlook

GET THERE Take IL-145 / IL-34 south from Harrisburg and turn left onto IL-34 S for 9.4 miles. Take a left onto 1180 N / Karbers Ridge Road and drive 2.8 miles.

Turn left on Garden of the Gods for 1.3 miles, then turn left to stay on Garden of the Gods Road for another 0.9 miles. The parking lot will be on your left.

Google Maps: bit.ly/timberindianpoint

RESTROOM At nearby picnic area or Observation Trail

FEE None

TREAT YOURSELF Grab some ice cream at the Garden of the Gods Outpost, located at the corner of Garden of the Gods and Karbers Ridge Road 2.4 miles from the trailhead.

Shawnee National Forest
(618) 253-7114
Facebook @shawneenatlforest

pond on the left that is teeming with frogs! Spend some time here and see how many species of wildlife you can find. Continue down the path to a fork. Go slightly right to reach Indian Point, an outcropping with views that stretch for miles overlooking the Shawnee National Forest. These unique rock formations were created by wind and rain over millions of years. The cliffs are steep, so use caution and don't go near the edges. This is a great place for a picnic lunch or power-up to enjoy the views. Continue along the path as it hugs the ledge, where you'll find several large rock overhangs and crevices to explore. Imagine a time when black bears lived in these woods. Do you think these shelter bluffs would make a good place for them to sleep? Don't worry, there aren't any bears in these woods anymore. After climbing uphill, you'll reach a fork. Continue straight as the trail narrows through ferns and shaded trees, and complete the loop back to the parking lot. There are many trails to explore in this region. Consider staying the weekend and camping nearby at Pharaoh Campground.

SCAVENGER HUNT

American bullfrog

As you approach the pond, listen for splashes as these carnivorous (eats meat) amphibians leap into the water from their perches along the edge or from lily pads. They can leap 3–6 feet. Pretend you're a frog and hop around the pond—can you leap 3 feet?

Lithobates catesbeianus

Seasonal special: cicada

These flying insects create the sound of summer. Males "sing" to attract females, and this loud metallic chorus is unmistakable. Can you find a live cicada, or an exoskeleton (the hard outer skin it sheds) on trees or plants?

A member of family Cicadoidea

Shelter bluffs

The rock surrounding you is 320 million years old and used to be covered by an ancient sea before being exposed to elements and slowly eroded away. Imagine what kind of animals might use these rock overhangs. Are you brave enough to explore them? Go inside and roar like a bear.

Many shelter bluffs to explore

Swiss cheese rocks

Look closely at the unusual rock formations along the trail. Do you see that some stones have small circles that look like Swiss cheese or honeycomb? This is caused by years of weathering and erosion. Draw these patterns in your nature journal.

These formations are called tafoni

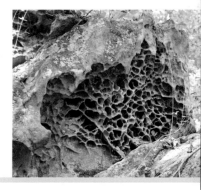

Seasonal special: late purple aster

Wildflowers are abundant in Shawnee National Forest from spring through fall. Spring has the most blooms, but late purple asters make their appearance in late summer. Look closely and see if you can count how many of the yellow disk flowers are in the middle and how many purple ray flowers/petals surround it. Which has more, the center or the petals?

Symphyotrichum patens

16

ROMP AROUND THE RIM ROCK NATIONAL RECREATIONAL TRAIL

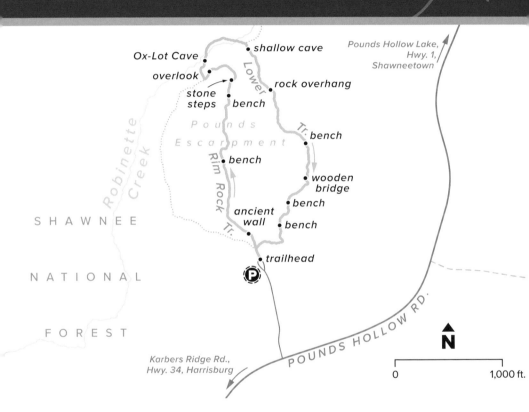

Pounds Hollow Lake, Hwy. 1, Shawneetown

shallow cave

Ox-Lot Cave

overlook

rock overhang

stone steps

bench

Lower

Pounds Escarpment

Tr.

bench

Robinette Creek

Rim Rock Tr.

bench

wooden bridge

bench

ancient wall

bench

trailhead

SHAWNEE

NATIONAL

FOREST

POUNDS HOLLOW RD.

Karbers Ridge Rd., Hwy. 34, Harrisburg

N

0   1,000 ft.

YOUR ADVENTURE

Adventurers, today you'll explore Rim Rock, a scenic trail recognized nationally for its beauty and archeological value. Archaeologists have found evidence that Native Americans once lived here over 2000 years ago; you are on the historical homeland of the Miami. You'll notice three trail options—head straight into the shaded trees along hand-laid flagstone on

The rock ledges of this trail are sure to impress →

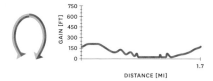

LENGTH 1.7-mile loop

ELEVATION GAIN 223 feet

HIKE TIME + EXPLORE 1.5 hours

DIFFICULTY Moderate—steep stairs down to the lower trail and back up

SEASON Year-round. Spring offers woodland flowers, and fall is glorious in this part of the forest.

GET THERE From Harrisburg, take IL-34 / IL-145 south to turn left on IL-34 south. In 9 miles, turn left onto Karbers Ridge Road and go 8.3 miles, then turn left into the Rim Rock parking lot and trailhead.

Google Maps: bit.ly/timberrimrocktrail

RESTROOM At trailhead

FEE None

TREAT YOURSELF Grab lunch at the Trails End Grill, located at the Double M campground about 5 miles from the trailhead.

Shawnee National Forest
(618) 253-7114
Facebook @shawneenatlforest

the Rim Rock trail. As you climb the stairs, look carefully for the remains of the ancient stone wall. It was built by the precontact people who lived here during the Late Woodland period (AD 600–900). Pass a maple tree and bench and reach a deck, where steep stairs take you down into a rock crevice and onto Lower Trail. Enter the narrow passageway covered in ferns and moss. Look around carefully; you might find some critters taking refuge. Continue through the crevice to the side of massive, impressive rock ledges. The trail can be a little obscured here, but go right and you'll easily find it leading down and around the rock ledge. You'll spot a streambed ahead to the left and Ox-Lot Cave to the right. Consider taking a power-up break here to look for minnows or other aquatic animals. Notice the blue blaze near the rock ledge. From here, you'll reach a junction with the Pounds Hollow Lake Trail to the left and the Lower Trail to the right—turn right on the Lower Trail and walk underneath impressive overhangs, past a bench, over a bridge, and past two more benches before coming to stairs that lead you back to the trailhead. There is a lot to explore in this region. Consider staying the weekend at the nearby Rim Rock's Dogwood Cabins or Double M Campground.

SCAVENGER HUNT

Ox-Lot Cave
Can you find Ox-Lot Cave? This massive overhang was once used by loggers in the early 1900s as a corral for oxen, mules, and horses. The oxen were used to drag logs out of the steep valley. Draw a scene in your nature journal of the cave holding the livestock.

An old corral

Black rat and ringneck snakes

Look carefully at the leaf litter and you might find these reptiles slithering by. While these two snakes are harmless, there are a couple venomous varieties living in these woods. Always use caution, observe from a distance, look before placing your hand or foot in rock crevices and over logs, and never touch. Can you smell with your tongue like a snake does?

Pantherophis obsoletus (left) and *Diadophis punctatus edwardsii* (right)

Seasonal special: hickory tussock caterpillar

Look closely at the moss-carpeted rocks and flowering plants to spot caterpillars. While spring is a great time to find them, some species like this black-and-white Hickory tussock moth larva appear in fall. Don't touch; woolly hair can irritate your skin. Look for signs of them munching on nearby leaves, just like the hungry, hungry caterpillar.

Lophocampa caryae

Seasonal special: pale touch-me-not

This pretty yellow jewelweed flower blooms from midsummer to fall. It is part of the flower family called touch-me-not. They get their funny name because if you touch a ripe seed pod, they explode, sending seeds in all directions. Give it a try—ball up like a seed pod and have a hike mate touch your head to make you spring to action!

Impatiens pallida

ADVENTURES IN
INDIANA

Adventurers, you'll head east from Illinois and enter the Hoosier State, founded in 1816, named so from a pioneer who would shout "Who's yere??" when they had visitors, and soon all Indianans used that phrase. You're on the historical homeland of Miami, as well as Potawatomi, Kickapoo, Shawnee, Peoria, Kaskaskia, and Adena culture. You'll begin in the southern part of the state in Hoosier National Forest—featuring old-growth forests, cliff bluffs, and waterfalls. Then you'll make your way along the scenic Ohio River byway, where you'll discover an island with historical ruins, before heading north toward the dense forests of the "Little Smokies" of Brown County. You'll explore both ancient cultures and pioneer history and trek along unique karst topography featuring caves, springs, and sinkholes. Then journey into deep canyons and ravines cut by glaciers and seemingly trapped in time. Continue north, exploring lakes, creeks, and nature preserves on your way to Indiana Dunes National Park along Lake Michigan. Embrace the Indiana state motto, "The Crossroads of America," as you hit the road. Enjoy!

17

CLIMB INTO THE CANYON AT HEMLOCK CLIFFS

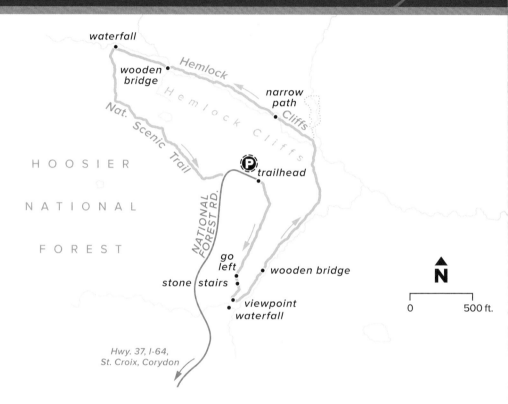

Map labels: waterfall, wooden bridge, Hemlock, narrow path, Hemlock Cliffs, Nat. Scenic Trail, trailhead, HOOSIER NATIONAL FOREST, NATIONAL FOREST RD., go left, stone stairs, wooden bridge, viewpoint waterfall, Hwy. 37, I-64, St. Croix, Corydon, N, 0, 500 ft.

YOUR ADVENTURE

Adventurers, today you'll be exploring a beautiful box canyon that is the historical home range of the Miami. Archaeologists have found evidence of human occupation in this canyon dating back 10,000 years. Follow the trail with white blazes at the end of the parking lot. Enter a thick canopied forest and then descend steep stairs into the canyon. Watch your footing because

This 60-foot seasonal waterfall is a key feature of the trail →

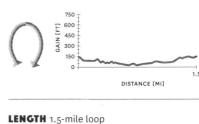

GAIN [FT]

750
600
450
300
150
0

1.5

DISTANCE [MI]

LENGTH 1.5-mile loop

ELEVATION GAIN 180 feet

HIKE TIME + EXPLORE 1–1.5 hours

DIFFICULTY Moderate—parts are steep and can be slick; small creek crossings

SEASON Year-round. Best in spring to see the waterfall flowing.

GET THERE From I-64, take Exit 79 toward French Lick. Follow IN-37 north 4 miles to turn right on Bethany Church Road. In 1.5 miles bear right on Mifflin-West Fork Road and follow to Hatfield Road, where you'll turn right for half a mile before turning left onto National Forest Road for 0.4 miles to the trailhead.

Google Maps: bit.ly/timberhemlockcliffs

RESTROOM At gas stations about 15 minutes south (where IN-37 and I-64 intersect)

FEE None

TREAT YOURSELF Try a pie at Schwartz Family Restaurant on IN-37, about 5 miles northwest.

Hoosier National Forest
(812) 547-7051
Facebook @HoosierNF

the stairs can be slick. When the trail splits, veer to the left. You may feel the air getting cooler as you descend. You'll emerge surrounded by rock overhangs, sandstone cliffs, and rock shelters. Do you notice the unusual honeycomb formation in the sandstone? Follow the trail past the upper viewing vantage point of a spectacularly tall, seasonal waterfall. It is show-iest during spring, which is also when wildflowers carpet the forest floor. Take the trail to the right to visit the bottom of the waterfall. Then head back up to the junction and go left, following the trail as it meanders over a bridge. There are fun creek crossings following the white blazes, so prepare to get a little wet and muddy when the water is high. The trail follows a babbling brook beneath a thick canopy of trees. Reach another creek crossing and a fork—stay left here, and be careful along a narrow drop. Cross another bridge and go uphill, past the cascade falls on your right. Then continue back to the parking lot. Consider camping nearby at the Indian-Celina Lakes Recreation Area.

SCAVENGER HUNT

Persimmon

The juicy orange fruits of this deciduous (loses its leaves) tree usually ripen in late September and can be eaten fresh, or used in breads, puddings, cakes, and beverages. Many species of wildlife enjoy the fruit. Have you ever tasted one?

Diospyros virginiana

Honeycomb stone

Look closely at the rock ledges to see unusual patterns. This Tar Springs Formation sandstone is roughly 350 million years old, part of the Mississippian system. Much of the sandstone is "honeycombed" by weathering of iron ores. What do the shapes look like to you?

Tafoni

Tulip tree fruit

This deciduous (loses its leaves) tree has flowers in spring that resemble tulips. They produce seeds in a cone-shaped fruit you can find during fall. The seeds are food for birds and mammals. Look for its pointy-lobed leaves and see how many lobes you can count.

Liriodendron tulipifera seed pod and flower

Wintergreen

Keep your eyes near the ground for this rare plant. It produces a white flower in spring and red berries in summer and fall, and its leaves stay green in winter. Historically, people made teas brewed from this plant to treat some medical ailments. Draw this special plant in your nature journal.

Gaultheria procumbens

Hemlocks

The area is named for this special tree that is rare in Indiana. Can you spot these tall evergreens that make small cones? Look closely—are the scales open or closed, green or brown? They open later in fall to disperse the seeds inside. If you find some fallen on the ground, see how many you can collect in one minute—then be sure to put them back.

Tsuga canadensis

18

TRAVEL PIONEER MOTHERS' MEMORIAL FOREST TRAIL

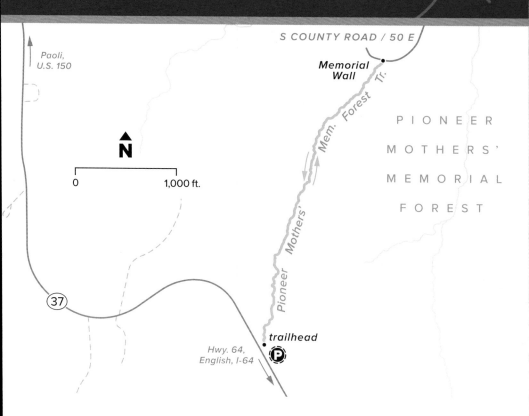

S COUNTY ROAD / 50 E

Paoli,
U.S. 150

Memorial
Wall

Mem. Forest Tr.

PIONEER

MOTHERS'

MEMORIAL

FOREST

N

0   1,000 ft.

Pioneer Mothers'

37

trailhead

Hwy. 64,
English, I-64

YOUR ADVENTURE

Adventurers, today you'll trek through a forest of giants with a storied history. This special place is one of the last old-growth forests in Indiana, on the historical homeland of the Kickapoo. Millions of acres of forest once covered the state, but nearly all were cut for lumber and farming in the 1800s. Joseph and Mary Cox purchased and protected this 88-acre

One of the only old-growth forests remaining in Indiana →

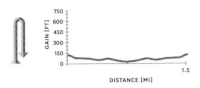

LENGTH 1.5-mile out and back

ELEVATION GAIN 125 feet

HIKE TIME + EXPLORE 1 hour

DIFFICULTY Easy—deeply shaded trail with very little elevation

SEASON Year-round. The forest is especially beautiful in fall, and spring flowers delight in April.

GET THERE Take IN-37 south through Paoli to the signed semicircle parking area on the east side of the road.

Google Maps: bit.ly/timberpioneermothers

RESTROOM At gas station 2 miles north in Paoli

FEE None

TREAT YOURSELF Try the homemade cobbler at Connie's Country Kitchen, located about 2 miles north on Main Street off IN-37.

Hoosier National Forest
(812) 547-7051
Facebook @HoosierNF

forest in 1816, never allowing any logging. Today, it's a nationally protected landmark. Archaeologists also discovered this forest was home to a walled village of precontact Native Americans; they lived here during the Oliver Phase from AD 1000 to 1500. While nothing remains of the ancient village, as you meander through the undisturbed woods, imagine what life might have been like two hundred years ago. How old do you think the trees around you are? Some ancient oaks have been standing here for centuries, while others have died and younger trees have replaced them. The trail leads to a memorial wall, built to thank the community that donated funds to protect the forest. When you reach the memorial wall, turn around and head back, or continue to Lick Creek. Make it a weekend and camp in a teepee or covered wagon at nearby Sleeping Bear Retreat.

SCAVENGER HUNT

Hickory tree pignuts

The pear-shaped nut from this deciduous (loses its leaves) tree can be found on the ground in September and October. They're called pignuts because pioneers fed them to their pigs. You may find the wood-like shells on the ground or just their husks. Can you juggle three or more at once?

Nuts from *Carya glabra*

Wood-decay fungus

Look at the forest floor and on dying trees and rotting wood to find a variety of colorful fungi. They serve an important role cleaning the forest and cycling nutrients back into the soil. There are 645 species in this family of fungi. How many kinds of mushrooms can you spot?

Meruliaceae

Beech fern

Did you know ferns are the oldest and one of the most diverse groups of plants? Fossil records date back over 300 million years. The entire leaf is called a frond. Look closer—you'll see the blade, the part with leaves (pinna) branching off, and look even closer—there are mini leaves on the pinna called pinnule. How many pinna and pinnule can you count on just one blade?

Phegopteris hexagonoptera

Wild turkeys

Did you know that wild turkeys were almost our national bird? The bald eagle won by just one vote. Turkeys used to be plentiful, but by the 1900s they could no longer be found in Indiana, due to loss of habitat and unregulated hunting. Thankfully, conservation efforts have restored wild turkey populations in the state. See if you can spot this large, impressive bird in the forest.

Meleagris gallopavo

Mighty oaks

This forest is home to species of oaks. Some of them are several hundred years old. Did you know that when squirrels find red oak acorns, they will

likely bury them to eat in winter or spring, but when they find white oak acorns, they will eat them immediately? Why do you think they do that?

Acorns from northern red oak (left) and black oak (right)

19

BE A ROSE ISLAND HISTORIAN AT CHARLESTOWN STATE PARK

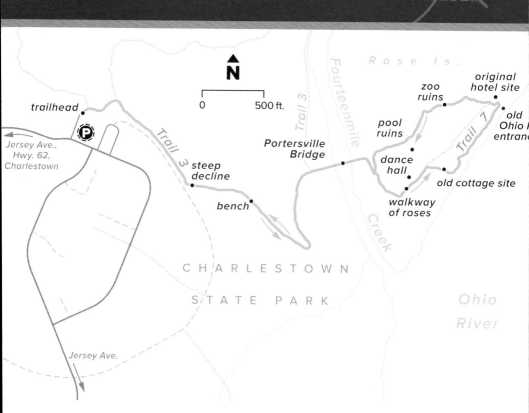

YOUR ADVENTURE

Adventurers, today you're going to hike Rose Island and explore an abandoned theme park from the 1920s, on the historical homeland of the Adena culture. You'll look for remains of the popular park that once welcomed thousands of people by steamship every summer before it was destroyed by the great flood of 1937. Today, a few building foundations, stone walkways,

Rose Island is an abandoned amusement park from 100 years ago →

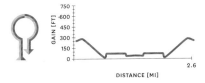

GAIN [FT]

750
600
450
300
150
0

DISTANCE [MI]

2.6

LENGTH 2.6-mile lollipop loop

ELEVATION GAIN 360 feet

HIKE TIME + EXPLORE 1.5–2 hours

DIFFICULTY Moderate—steep walk down and back up paved path that leads to and from Rose Island

SEASON Year-round, though summer can be hot and muggy.

GET THERE Follow the Ohio River Scenic Byway / IN-62 north from downtown Charlestown to turn right on Jersey Ave. Stay right and follow about 2 miles to turn left into the Charlestown State Park entrance. Turn left at the sign for Trailhead 3 and Rose Island and park in the lot.

Google Maps: bit.ly/timberroseisland

RESTROOM At state park campground

FEE $7 for Indiana residents (annual passes available); $9 for nonresidents

TREAT YOURSELF King Donuts on Market Street is about 2 miles from the park.

Charlestown State Park
(812) 256-5600
Facebook @Charlestownsp

and a concrete swimming pool are all that remain as nature reclaims the land. Begin your journey by staying to the right on a steep walk down the paved path on Trail 3. Power up at a bench if you need it. Stay right on Trail 7 before crossing a historical bridge over Fourteen Mile Creek that leads to Rose Island. Take a right through a grand entry welcoming you to stroll through nature and history. As you walk, notice the flood markers and see how many ruins you can find. One of the most prominent is an old swimming pool. How many trees and wildflowers are growing where structures like a dining hall, cabins, and a resort once stood? Stroll through the old Walkway of Roses and enjoy views of the Ohio River. Come to the old entry gates along the river. Try to imagine what it was like to arrive here by steamship. Then head under an arch and follow the trail to look for the remnants of an old zoo. Follow the path back to the historical bridge and climb back to the trailhead. Consider camping at the Charlestown State Park Campground and exploring more trails.

SCAVENGER HUNT

Historical bridge

This bridge was dismantled from its original location and relocated to Charlestown State Park, opening to the public in 2011. Look closely at its structure—these are called trusses that support the weight of the bridge. Try sketching the shape of the trusses in your nature journal and ponder why engineers built it this way.

Portersville Bridge was built in 1912

Global fungi

This family of fungi grows on rocks in every continent of the world! They are lichenized, which means they have formed a symbiotic (partnership) relationship with species of algae or bacteria to form a lichen. Do you have a symbiotic relationship with anyone where you both benefit from it?

A member of family Umbilicariaceae

Cherry bug

Look but don't touch! These are the biggest milli-pedes in this region. They are colorful and named for the scent they emit through pores along the sides of their body—it smells like almonds or sweet cherries. This is actually a poisonous chemical the millipede uses to defend itself from predators. What do they smell like to you?

Apheloria virginiensis corrugata (means "wrinkled" in Latin)

Amusement park ruins

Stroll the old walkway of roses and try to imagine these arches covered with

hundreds of fragrant flowers. Then climb the ladder into what remains of the old swimming pool. What three things do you think are different today than they were for children one hundred years ago?

The Walkway of Roses

CHASE WATERFALLS AT CLIFTY FALLS STATE PARK

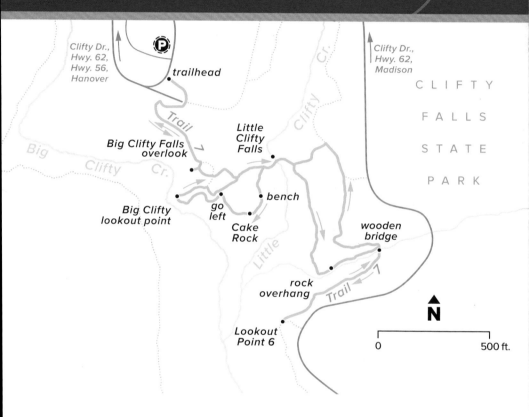

YOUR ADVENTURE

Adventurers, today you'll explore Trail 7 and take in views of some of the tallest waterfalls in Indiana, on the historical homeland of the Miami. Your journey begins with an awe-inspiring view of Big Clifty Falls. The trail hugs the ridgeline, offering beautiful views of the ravine and creek below. Take the trail left toward Little Clifty Falls. Reach an intersection and go

60-foot Big Clifty Falls is one of Indiana's tallest →

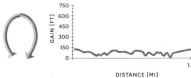

LENGTH 1.1-mile loop

ELEVATION GAIN 266 feet

HIKE TIME + EXPLORE 1.5 hours

DIFFICULTY Moderate—rugged terrain and elevation changes

SEASON Year-round. From December to June, the waterfalls are at their fullest.

GET THERE From IN-7, head north on IN-62 / Clifty Drive. Go 3 miles, then turn right into Clifty Falls State Park North Gate. The parking lot for the trailhead is directly ahead.

Google Maps: bit.ly/timbercliftyfalls

RESTROOM At trailhead (in late fall and winter, nearest at Clifty Falls Inn)

FEE $7 day fee for Indiana residents (annual passes available); $9 day fee for nonresidents. Admission free during winter.

TREAT YOURSELF Get a scoop or two at Scoop's Ice Cream on Main Street in downtown Madison.

Clifty Falls State Park
(812) 273-8885
Facebook @CliftyFallsSP

left and down the stairs where the boardwalk goes directly over the falls. Look down—how tall do you think this waterfall is? Cross to the other side of the ravine to another intersection. Go right to take the trail over a bridge to Lookout Tower 6, which offers a lovely view of Big Clifty Falls and the valley. Continue on the trail, heading back toward Little Clifty Falls. Cross a bridge over a small waterfall and follow the trail back across the bridge over the falls. This time when you reach the intersection, go left down stairs, power up on a bench, and follow the trail along the ridge toward Cake Rock. Turn left to find another viewpoint of Big Clifty Falls. Turn left again on the main trail to end up back at the trailhead. There are many trails to explore in this park. Consider making it a weekend and staying at the Clifty Inn or campground in Clifty Falls State Park.

SCAVENGER HUNT

Seasonal special: wild columbine

This beautiful plant is named after eagles and doves. The Latin word *aquila* means "eagle," referencing the claw-like spurs at the base of the flower. *Columbine* comes from the Latin word for "dove" because the inverted flower looks like doves clustered together. Look for blooms in May along the rocks and cliffs, especially near Cake Rock.

Aquilegia canadensis

Eastern red cedar

This evergreen tree, which stays green year-round, may be most easily identified by its blue berry-like cones with seeds inside that birds and other wildlife eat. Look closely at its leaves—they are scalier than other conifers (trees with cones). Try sketching one in your nature journal.

Juniperus virginiana

Cake Rock

Try to find this unusual rock formation. Cake Rock is limestone, believed to be a glacial deposit left behind by the Illinoian glacier. While it is unknown how old this rock is, the Illinoian stage was between 300,000 to 140,000 years ago. Naturalists know it has been here a very long time because of the plant life growing on it. Lichens, moss, and ferns are some of the oldest plants on Earth, and they cover Cake Rock. Why do you think it was given that name?

Cake Rock

Little Clifty Falls

Do you think this waterfall is taller or shorter than Big Clifty Falls? Surprise! They are both 60 feet. It runs off of Little Clifty Creek, a tributary of Big Clifty Creek that flows into the 981-mile-long Ohio River, which flows into the 2340-mile-long Mississippi River and ends in the Gulf of Mexico—drop a leaf in and imagine it going all the way to the Gulf.

One of the tallest falls in Indiana

Oak leaves

There are many different species of this deciduous (loses its leaves) tree. All have similar but uniquely shaped leaves with a different number of lobes/sections. What is similar and different about these oak leaves?

Scarlet oak (right) and white oak (left)

21

WALK THE BLUFFS OF BEAVER BEND

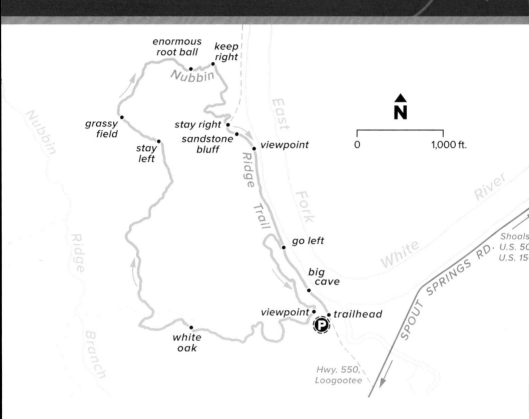

YOUR ADVENTURE

Adventurers, today you'll climb to the Bluffs of Beaver Bend for a bird's-eye view of the river below, and walk through a shaded hardwood forest that is the historical home of the Miami. Start down the gravel path from the parking area, passing massive bluffs of Mansfield Sandstone. Notice the varied coloration of stone and unique patterns caused by years of weathering.

View of the East Fork White River →

GAIN [FT]

750
600
450
300
150
0

2.9

DISTANCE [MI]

LENGTH 2.9-mile loop

ELEVATION GAIN 371 feet

HIKE TIME + EXPLORE 2 hours

DIFFICULTY Moderate—longer, with a tough climb at the beginning to the top of the bluffs

SEASON Year-round. April and May have spring flowers; fall has changing leaves. Winter offers less-obstructed views of the river and rocks.

GET THERE Take Water Street south through Shoals to where it becomes Sprout Springs Road. In 0.8 miles take your first right and drive 0.2 miles to the parking lot and trailhead.

Google Maps: bit.ly/timberbluffs

RESTROOM At gas station in Shoals, about 1.5 miles from trailhead

FEE None

TREAT YOURSELF Get a sundae at Bo-Mac's Drive Inn, about 1.5 miles from the trail.

Bluffs of Beaver Bend
(812) 737-2087
Facebook @TNCIndiana
Facebook @INDNR

Find the trailhead for the Nubbin Ridge Trail on the left. It's a steep climb, but worth it when you reach the top of the bluffs you were just admiring and see the East Fork White River below. After the lookout, go right at the trail marker. There aren't many trail blazes, but the trail is easy to follow. As you journey through the forest, notice the diversity of mushrooms, ferns, wildflowers, and trees. Look closely in the canopy for birds that live or travel through here. Conservationists found a "shell mound"—remnants of freshwater mussels from the river below—on the bluff, indicating they were a major food source for native peoples, who also fashioned the shells into tools and ornaments. Pass enormous ancient oak trees and young saplings. The Nature Conservancy has been working to restore areas of this forest. Go left at a trail marker and reach an open meadow with native grasses. Right along the trail, find an enormous fallen tree. Size yourself up to the root ball and guess the tree's age, then head back toward the ridgeline and turn right. Pass enormous bluffs across the ravine to your right and see additional river views. Turn right at the next trail marker and descend down to the trail exit. Turn right at the bottom and return to the parking lot. Consider camping nearby at the Martin State Forest Campground.

SCAVENGER HUNT

Honeycomb sandstone

How many shapes and patterns can you find in the ancient sandstone? Notice the varied coloration, which is unique for this area. Draw the patterns of the stone in your nature journal. When you get home, color it in, trying to match the color variation you see.

Mansfield sandstone is about 300 million years old

Stump puffball

These strange-looking fungi grow in clusters on decaying tree stumps. They can look like little balls or deflated balloons. In fall they expel a gray dust from a hole in the top. The dust is actually spores, or seeds, to help make new puffballs. If you find one, give it a gentle squeeze and see what happens.

Lycoperdon pyriforme

Wood blue aster

These pretty blue flowers are part of the sunflower family. They bloom in late summer to early fall. The name *aster* comes from a word meaning "star," for the starlike shape of the flower heads. Look closely—the center is actually several mini flowers called flowerets. How many flowerets can you count?

Symphyotrichum cordifolium

Sassafras

This deciduous (loses its leaves) tree is sometimes called mitten tree because of the shape of its leaves, which come in three shapes: mitten-

shaped, three-lobed, and ovate. If you find sassafras leaves on the ground, crush them a bit—what do they smell like? Some think they have a faint Froot Loops aroma. The root of this plant was the original flavor source for root beer.

Sassafras albidum

22

COAST THE KARST TRAIL AT SPRING MILL STATE PARK

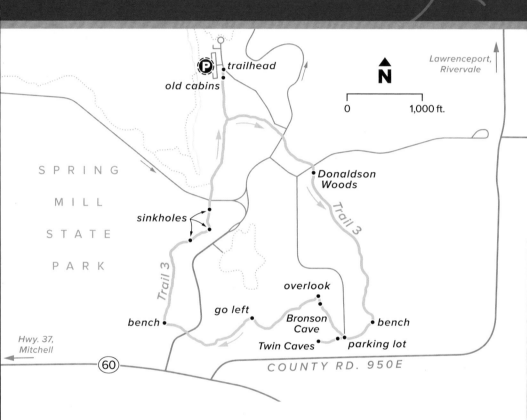

SPRING MILL STATE PARK

Lawrenceport, Rivervale

trailhead

old cabins

Donaldson Woods

Trail 3

sinkholes

Trail 3

overlook

go left

bench

Bronson Cave

bench

Twin Caves

parking lot

Hwy. 37, Mitchell

60

COUNTY RD. 950E

N

0   1,000 ft.

YOUR ADVENTURE

Adventurers, today you'll navigate a unique terrain called karst, on the historical homeland of the Miami; there are sinkholes, streams, caves, and springs. Start on Trail 3, spotting two old cabins on the left. Go left at a fork. Power up at a bench if needed, and turn left for Donaldson Woods, named for George Donaldson. In the mid-1800s, when most of Indiana was cleared

Don't miss this restored Pioneer Village →

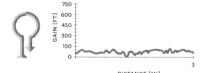

DISTANCE [MI]

LENGTH 3-mile lollipop loop

ELEVATION GAIN 259 feet

HIKE TIME + EXPLORE 2 hours

DIFFICULTY Moderate—longer, with rugged terrain and a bit of elevation

SEASON Year-round.

GET THERE From IN-37 in Mitchell, take IN-60 east for 3.4 miles to turn left into Spring Mill State Park. Turn left at the Spring Mill Inn sign to head into the upper parking lot. You'll see Trail 3 access on the left, just before entering the parking lot.

Google Maps:
bit.ly/timberspringmilltrailhead3

RESTROOM At Spring Mill Inn and on trail near Twin Caves

FEE $7 day fee for Indiana residents (annual passes available); $9 for nonresidents

TREAT YOURSELF Grab a banana split, sundae, or milkshake just down the road at Dairy Bell.

Spring Mill State Park
(812) 849-3534
Facebook @Springmillsp

for timber and farming, he never allowed this forest to be cut, which is why it's considered "old-growth." Filled with massive oak, hickory, and beech trees, it's one of the few uncut forests left in Indiana, a National Natural Landmark. Cross a road, pass a massive downed tree, cross another road, and walk through a short section of the woods to reach a parking lot. Pass under the stone archway and down stairs to Twin Caves. Guided tours are sometimes offered. Look at the unique cave entryways and river that flows between them, then climb the stairs to continue on Trail 3, to the left of the restroom. The trail descends to Bronson Cave. There is a bench and a walkway to view the cave. After taking it in, head back up to the trail and turn right. At a wayfinder sign, go left. Cross another road, then pass a bench and sinkholes on both sides. Look far off to the left to see a massive sinkhole. Cross yet another road and turn right to stay on Trail 3 and return to the trailhead. Consider staying at Spring Mill Inn or the nearby campground and check out the preserved Pioneer Village down the road.

SCAVENGER HUNT

Seasonal special: Kentucky warbler
These forests attract many bird species. In spring and summer, look in the trees for brilliant flashes of yellow, red, or blue. Forest birds like scarlet tanagers, Kentucky warblers, and blue jays like to visit here. See if you can whistle like a songbird.

Geothlypis formosa

Bonnet mushrooms
There are over 10,000 different types of mushrooms. Can you find one that looks like it's wearing a little cap? Look under the small bonnets for its gills, which help the mushroom make spores to reproduce—how many gills you can spot on just one mushroom?

Mycena galericulata

Cave and wheel

The sinkholes create caves throughout this park. Twin Caves had its ceiling collapse to expose an underground stream, known as a "karst window." Can you find the wheel? It adjusts the water level of the stream in Twin Caves for guided boat tours. What kind of boat would you design to enter these caves?

Twin Caves and a wheel

Pawpaw trees

Pawpaws are North America's largest native fruit-bearing tree. They produce large, yellow-greenish fruit in spring that's sweet and has a custard-like flavor, similar to a mix of mango and banana. They can be eaten raw, but are also good in desserts. Would you try pawpaw ice cream?

Asimina triloba ("tri" because of its three-lobed leaves)

Northern red oak

Look for one of the massive oaks in Donaldson Woods; they are hundreds of years old. Red oak leaves have 7–11 lobes with a pointy bristle tip. Trace one in your nature journal, then try to find another type of oak during this walk and trace its leaf to compare.

Quercus rubra

23

STROLL THE "LITTLE SMOKIES" IN BROWN COUNTY STATE PARK

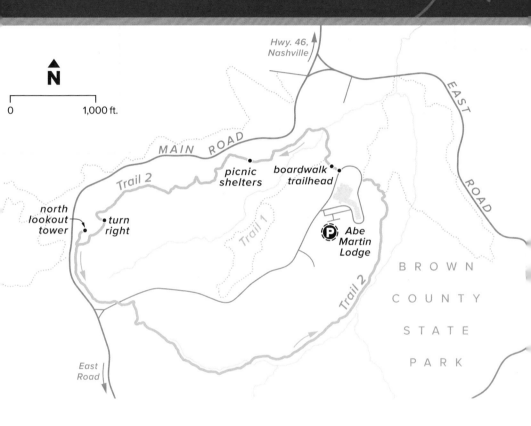

YOUR ADVENTURE

Adventurers, today you'll explore Trail 2, also known as the Civilian Conservation Corps (CCC) Trail, in Indiana's largest state park and the historical homeland of the Miami. This forested beauty has been called the "Little Smokies" for its rugged hills, ravines, and immense forests that resemble a smaller version of the Great Smoky Mountains. This historical trail

Enjoy nature along this historical trail →

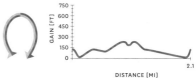

GAIN [FT]

750
600
450
300
150
0

2.1

DISTANCE [MI]

LENGTH 2.1-mile loop

ELEVATION GAIN 322 feet

HIKE TIME + EXPLORE 1.5–2 hours

DIFFICULTY Moderate—rugged terrain and some elevation

SEASON Year-round, but the colors in fall are exquisite.

GET THERE Take IN-46 east from Bloomington to turn right onto IN-135 S / IN-46 E. In 1.7 miles, turn right onto Brown County State Park Road. Enter the North Gatehouse entrance and head straight for 1.4 miles, following signs for Abe Martin Lodge & Cabins. Turn left toward the lodge and follow to the parking lot. The trailhead is behind the lodge. Note: North Gatehouse entrance is for small vehicles. There is a covered bridge with 9-foot clearance. If you're driving a larger vehicle or towing a trailer, use the West Gate entrance.

Google Maps: bit.ly/timberbrowncounty2

RESTROOM At lodge

FEE $7 for Indiana residents (annual passes available); $9 for nonresidents

TREAT YOURSELF Try out local honey, syrups, or pies from Nashville General Store & Bakery, about 4 miles away in downtown Nashville.

Brown County State Park
(812) 988-6406
Facebook @BrownCountyStatePark

features stone stairs, bridges, retaining walls, and shelters built by the CCC in the 1930s. Begin behind the Abe Martin Lodge and go counterclockwise on a boardwalk, then descend stairs and turn right. Go down more stone stairs before crossing a bridge, descending additional stairs, and crossing a bridle trail (horse trail). The trail parallels the bridle trail, so don't be surprised to see horses in the woods. Reach an event shelter, follow the trail left, and pass a playground. Cross a small bridge and keep left at the way-finder sign. Pass shelters on the right, a stone bridge, and descend into the ravine. Turn right, crossing a bridle trail before reaching a lookout tower on your right. This is about the halfway point. Climb the stairs and enter the shelter for a sweeping forest view and a power-up on the benches. Continue through the forest, crossing a road into the ravine over two bridges, a bench, and back up. Pass cabins on the left before returning to the Abe Martin Lodge, taking a left at the final trail junction. Consider staying at the lodge or camping nearby at the Buffalo Ridge Campground to explore more trails.

SCAVENGER HUNT

Bridle trails

There are 70 miles of horse trails in Brown County State Park. Can you find evidence that horses might have crossed this path? Look in the dirt or mud for prints, and keep your eye out for horses on the trail.

Horseshoe in mud

Count the rings

Want to know how old a tree is? Count the rings. What do you think the world was like when this tree was a seedling?

One ring equals one year in a tree's life

Viewpoint

Take in the view of Indiana's knob terrain from this lookout tower. The Knobstone Escarpment is the most rugged terrain in Indiana. Its most

prominent features are the steep hills, called knobs, and ravines. Brown County State Park features views from the region's highest elevations. How many stairs do you have to climb to the lookout to see this incredible terrain from up there?

North lookout tower

Gilled mushroom

Look for mushrooms with fleshy flaps that look like fish gills. They are used to make spores (or seeds) to reproduce. If you find a fallen mushroom, separate the cap from the stalk and put the cap on a piece of white paper. Get the cap a little bit wet and cover it with a glass overnight. In the morning, you should see a spore print—that's how many spores a mushroom lets go of!

Hydnangiaceae

Eastern chipmunk

These forest-foraging rodents are abundant on the trail. Did you know they have fur-lined cheek pouches they can fill with food the size of their head? Puff your cheeks out as much as you can. What do you think you could store in there?

Tamias striatus

24

STALK WOLF CAVE AT MCCORMICK'S CREEK STATE PARK

YOUR ADVENTURE

Adventurers, today you'll be rock hopping, creek crossing, and cave crawl-ing on the historical homeland of Miami. Start at the nature center to learn about the park's natural features. Then find Trail 5, also called Wolf Cave Trail, and follow it through shaded woods, looking for sinkholes. Go slightly left to stay on Trail 5, and power up at a bench. Cross a bridge, pass a couple

Bring a headlamp and explore Wolf Cave →

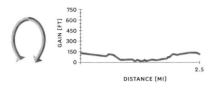

LENGTH 2.5-mile loop

ELEVATION GAIN 200 feet

HIKE TIME + EXPLORE 2 hours

DIFFICULTY Moderate—longer, with a couple creek of crossings

SEASON Year-round. Late summer to early fall offers the best conditions for exploring the cave (drier, less muddy).

GET THERE From Bloomington, take IN-46 west and turn right at the McCormick's Creek State Park sign. Follow Park Road to the trailhead. There is a small parking lot located at Trailhead 5, and another one around the corner near Pine Bluff shelter.

Google Maps: bit.ly/timberwolfcave

RESTROOM At Pine Bluff shelter near trailhead

FEE $7 day fee for Indiana residents (annual passes available); $9 for nonresidents

TREAT YOURSELF Get a cone from Grand's Ice Cream just outside the park entrance.

McCormick's Creek State Park
(812) 829-2235
Facebook @McCormickscreeksp

of benches, and cross a creek to arrive at Wolf Cave. Wolves once lived in Indiana, and many years ago, this cave was home to a pack. Use a headlamp or flashlight and have a look around. When you're done, stay right at the junction, come to a boardwalk, and find Twin Bridges, two natural arches. The path follows a gentle creek with multiple crossings, and a small cascade offers a delightful spot to power up. The trail will climb, but there are several benches for resting. When you intersect Trail 8, turn left and then slightly right to stay on Trail 5. End at the road near the parking lot, a few hundred feet from where you started. Consider making a weekend of it and staying at the park's campground.

SCAVENGER HUNT

Cave spiders

There are about four hundred species of spiders living in Indiana, but only some have adapted to living in caves, which are dark, humid, and

food-limited. Cave spiders that have lived many generations in caves evolve to lose their pigment. Some even lose their eyesight. Shine your flashlight on the ceiling to find a spider. What does it look like? How is it alike or different from other spiders you've seen?

Some spiders are cave specialists

Sinkholes

Look for bowl-shaped depressions called sinkholes, which are formed as the limestone bedrock is slowly removed from beneath the soil, due to water moving underground. This slowly dissolves the limestone and forms an underground network of passageways to carry the water.

Some sinkholes are small, and some are large, in groups or rows

Find the fungi

Fungi is fabulous, and there are hundreds of kinds in Indiana. Some look like shelves on trees, others grow to the size of soccer balls, while others are

almost microscopic. Their shape and color vary, but they all have an important job: cleaning up dead trees and cycling nutrients back into the soil. How many shapes, sizes, colors, and textures of fungi can you find? Write a haiku about mushrooms.

Bracket fungi

Bats

Thirteen species of these small mammals have been identified in Indiana, including the little brown bat. Six species use caves and mines in winter, and four species can be found in summer and during spring and fall migration. Many are considered rare or endangered. Inside Wolf Cave during summer, you might spot a bat tucked up in small cracks in the rocks sleeping. If you see one, do not disturb it. What other animals sleep during the day and wake up at night?

Myotis lucifugus

Natural bridges

Around 250 million years ago, this area was covered by a shallow sea. Limy mud and sand were deposited layer by layer on the sea bottom. As they became buried, they were compressed into layers of solid limestone. Here, it eventually collapsed from water flow to create these natural bridges. Howl like a wolf when you find one!

Natural bridges

25

SPOT ENDANGERED BATS AT SODALIS NATURE PARK

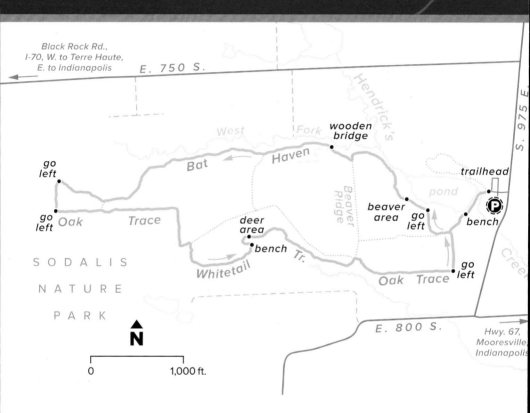

YOUR ADVENTURE

Adventurers, today you'll explore a 210-acre nature park on the historical homeland of the Miami, taking several trails that create a loop. Cross the bridge near the small cascade and walk the path along the pond, past a bench. At a fork, go slightly right. At another fork with a wayfinder sign, turn right onto Beaver Ridge Trail. Walk through mature forests toward the pond.

Explore four unique trails near Sodalis pond →

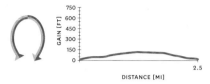

DISTANCE [MI]

LENGTH 2.5-mile loop

ELEVATION GAIN 72 feet

HIKE TIME + EXPLORE 1.5–2 hours

DIFFICULTY Easy—flat, well-marked trails

SEASON Year-round, but summer is recommended to spot the endangered bats the park is named after. Consider visiting in late afternoon and staying till dusk to observe bats near the pond.

GET THERE From Indianapolis, take I-70 west to Exit 66 toward Mooresville, turn left off the exit then left again on IN-267 S for 1.1 miles, then go left on E County Road 750 S. In 1.2 miles, turn right on S County Road 975 E and find the parking lot on your right.

Google Maps: bit.ly/timbersodalis

RESTROOM At trailhead

FEE None

TREAT YOURSELF Enjoy a fun atmosphere and sweets at Chunky Monkey Ice Cream and Sweets, about 5 miles south on IN-67 in Mooresville.

Sodalis Nature Park
(317) 839-7665
Facebook @PlainfieldParksandRec

The trail curves left, passing a bench and following the pond's edge. Look closely for evidence of beavers. Follow the trail to Bat Haven connector and go right. This trail is more rugged and narrow, with some tree roots. Cross small bridges and streams and pass a couple of trail connectors. Stay straight on Bat Haven Trail until you must turn left. At the next wayfinder sign, go left onto Oak Trace Trail. Walk through a forest of oaks along this path. When you reach the connector for Whitetail Trail, turn right. There is a picnic bench and open woodland—keep your eyes out for white-tailed deer here. When you reach the Oak Trace connector, turn right and follow it to the next wayfinder sign, where you will go left, staying on Oak Trace. This will lead back to the first trail connection near the pond's edge. Turn right and head back to the trailhead.

SCAVENGER HUNT

Beaver

These rodents (mammals with teeth that continuously grow) are active in the park. They specifically like the cherry trees, and you can see their handiwork near the pond on Beaver Ridge Trail. How many trees can you count that have been chewed or felled by beaver? Why do you think they chew trees?

Evidence of beavers

White-tailed deer

These mammals are shy and primarily a crepuscular species, which means they are most active during dusk and dawn. When scared, they run and warn others in their herd of potential danger by raising their tail and flashing the white fur. How do you alert your family if you feel scared?

Odocoileus virginianus

Indiana bat

This park was named for this small, endangered mammal that roosts here in summer and raises pups (baby bats). The trees along Bat Haven Trail support a maternity colony of female bats. Try to spot them at dusk near the pond, feasting on night-flying insects like moths, mosquitos, and midges. Put three pennies in your hand—that's how much this tiny bat weighs.

Myotis sodalis

Panicled aster

From spring to fall, you can find wildflowers and the pollinators that love them, like bees, butterflies, and flies. Wildflowers like aster prefer sunshine, while other species thrive in deep shade. Count how many different flowers you can find. Use Seek or your favorite nature identification app on your smartphone, and keep a list in your nature journal of how many species you find.

Symphyotrichum lanceolatum

Northern red oak

Look up and you might just spot this deciduous (loses its leaves) tree with dark gray or brown bark and dark green leaves with 7–11 sharp lobes. Their acorns have a reddish-brown cup on one end that stays on the tree through winter. Collect as many acorn caps as you can from the ground, cover your fingers with them, and wiggle them at your hike mates.

Quercus rubra

26

TIME TRAVEL IN TURKEY RUN STATE PARK

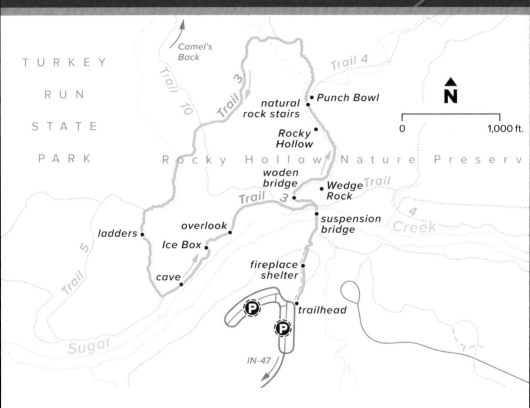

YOUR ADVENTURE

Adventurers, today you're exploring rugged Trail 3 that will feel like you're in prehistoric Indiana. Hike the Rocky Hollow stream through deep fern- and moss-covered gorges and experience the last remnants of magnificent forest that once covered most of Indiana. This landscape is a nationally recognized natural landmark and was once home to the Miami. Begin by

Step back in time on this extraordinary trail →

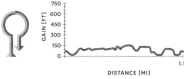

LENGTH 1.9-mile lollipop loop

ELEVATION GAIN 394 feet

HIKE TIME + EXPLORE 2–2.5 hours

DIFFICULTY Challenging—very rugged trail with ladders; can modify for little hikers by taking Trail 3 to Trail 10 connection (but it's still "moderate")

SEASON Year-round. Spring rains can mean higher water and tougher hiking conditions; icicles and frozen waterfalls are beautiful in winter.

GET THERE From Indianapolis, take I-74 W to Exit 52 and turn left on IN-75 S. Travel 1.9 miles, then continue on IN-234 W / W 800 S / County Line Road for 19 miles. Turn left on IN-47S for 13.7 miles. Turn right onto Park Road and find Turkey Run Nature Center on your right; the trailhead is located behind it.

Google Maps: bit.ly/timberturkeyrun

RESTROOM At trailhead

FEE $7 for Indiana residents (annual passes available); $9 day fee for nonresidents.

TREAT YOURSELF Grab some sweets at Gobbler's Knob Sweets, Eats & Mercantile, 2 miles down the road on Hwy 41.

Turkey Run State Park
(765) 597-2635
Facebook @TurkeyRunandShades

descending seventy stairs and crossing a suspension bridge over Sugar Creek to enter the preserve. Stay right on Trail 3 over another bridge, as you enter a sensitive biological area with multiple creek crossings. Reach a small cascade, climb a log, and follow the streambed. When you reach the Punch Bowl, go left to stay on Trail 3. Follow the creek to stairs, and stay left at the next junction with Trail 10. Climb stairs up, cross a bridge, and take more stairs down and back up. At another junction, stay straight for Trail 3, unless you're tired and want to head left on Trail 10 as a shortcut. Descend more stairs, staying left at the bottom, and take three ladders down carefully. At another junction with Trail 5, stay left, passing a cool cave. Then take another left, follow the stone stairs up, and you'll see the Ice Box, a circular glacial formation, to the right. Power up at benches at an overlook of Sugar Creek, then stay right once you pass Trail 10 on the left. At the suspension bridge, turn right back to the trailhead. Consider staying the night at the Turkey Run Inn or at the park campgrounds and hitting the trail early to avoid crowds.

SCAVENGER HUNT

Bryophytes

Bryophytes, which includes liverworts and mosses, are some of the most ancient plants on land. Nearly 50 percent of all the bryophytes species that

have been found in Indiana live right here within Rocky Hollow. They have lived on the canyon walls and floor for thousands of years. It's important to protect them by staying off the rocks so they are undisturbed. How many different kinds can you find?

Thuidium delicatulum (left) and *Conocephalum conicum* (right)

Climb stone stairs

In the narrow canyons, look around: can you spot stairs carved into the sandstone to help your journey? If you are hiking when water is high, these stairs will come in handy. It's a mystery who carved these stairs, but they have been here for about one hundred years. They are smooth and worn from millions of footsteps. How many stairs can you count?

Stairs carved into stone generations ago

Punchbowl

Can you find the large pothole known as the Punchbowl? Potholes are formed by boulders (called erratics) that were carried here from Canada by glaciers. They got caught in swirling water, and their tumbling chiseled down the soft sandstone, leaving circular formations. How big do you think the boulder was that caused the Punchbowl?

A glacial pothole carved by melting glaciers

Colorful canyon

Look closely at the canyon walls. Can you find areas that look like they have been painted with yellow, orange, and red watercolors? That's not paint—it's minerals! Iron turns to rust when it comes into contact with oxygen, leaving color-ful streaks. Take a photo, and when you get home, make a painting of the canyon wall using watercolors.

Minerals paint the canyon walls

27

DISCOVER THE SECRET SPLENDOR OF SHADES STATE PARK

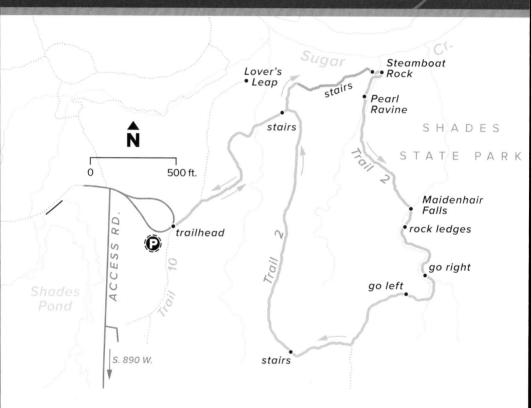

YOUR ADVENTURE

Adventurers, today you'll hike a spectacular trail that begins in a peaceful forest with trees so large it takes two or more people to wrap their arms around them. This is the historical homeland of the Miami. Its landscape is similar to Turkey Run State Park nearby. Both were cut by glaciers tens of thousands of years ago and are unlike anywhere else in Indiana. Follow the

Explore ravines and sandstone canyons in this extraordinary landscape →

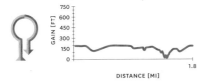

GAIN [FT]

750
600
450
300
150
0

1.8

DISTANCE [MI]

LENGTH 1.8-mile lollipop loop

ELEVATION GAIN 246 feet

HIKE TIME + EXPLORE 1–1.5 hours

DIFFICULTY Challenging—many steep stairs and trekking along a creek bed with uneven surfaces that can be muddy and slick; best suited for older children

SEASON Year-round, but high waters in spring can lead to trail closures. August and September are driest. Fall has wonderful colors and fewer visitors than nearby Turkey Run.

GET THERE Take IN-47 south from Crawfordsville to turn right on IN-234. In 5 miles turn left onto W 800 S for 0.8 miles, then right onto S 890 W for 0.3 miles. Turn right to enter Shades State Park, veering slightly left on Shades Lake Road for 0.2 miles. Park in the lot near the Dell shelter to reach Trailhead #2.

Google Maps: bit.ly/timbershades2

RESTROOM At parking lot

FEE $7 day fee for Indiana residents (annual passes available); $9 day fee for nonresidents. If you plan to visit both Shades State Park and nearby Turkey Run State Park during the same day, you only need to pay the day fee once—just be sure to save your receipt so you can show it at the gatehouse.

TREAT YOURSELF Get a root beer float or an ice cream cone at Sweet Country Cream, about 5 miles south of the park.

Shades State Park
(765) 435-2810
Facebook @TurkeyRunandShades

path toward Trail 2 and Lover's Leap, staying right at the junction toward Trail 2. Cross a bridge and climb some stairs. At the fork, go left. Make your way through the forest and down a steep staircase with 160 stairs to find Steamboat Rock at the bottom. Follow the creek bed—lined with ferns, mosses, and lichen—through Pearl Ravine, a sandstone canyon with enormous rock ledges, on your way to the elegant Maidenhair Falls. Climb the stairs toward the falls, and follow the trail along the creek with impressive rock ledges. It will lead to the right, where you'll climb steep stairs and follow the trail toward the left. Cross more bridges and climb more stairs up and down as you traverse the rolling hills through tranquil forest. Listen carefully. Do you hear a raucous caucus of crows or songbirds? Or the faint sound of scuffling among leaves as squirrels hunt for nuts? Reach the first junction and turn left to return to the trailhead. Consider making a weekend of it by staying at one of the campgrounds in the park.

SCAVENGER HUNT

Christmas fern

Any guesses why this fern is named Christmas? Because parts of its leaves remain green through Christmastime. Feel its leathery pinnae, or leaves (*pinnae* means "feathers" in Latin)—how do they look different than other ferns' pinnae? What other plants are green during winter holidays?

Polystichum acrostichoides

Seersucker sedge

This shade-loving plant thrives in moist, rich, shaded soils. Can you find its bright green, waxy leaves among the ferns and mosses in the ravines and canyon? It's also called crinkle-leaf sedge— does it look like strips of wrinkled laundry to you?

Carex plantaginea

Seasonal special: morel hunting

All Indiana state parks allow morel hunting. On Trail 2, you'll have the best luck on the southern portion of the trail. These spongy, cone-shaped mushrooms arrive in mid- to late spring among the dead leaves at the foot of trees, especially oak, elm, and ash. They are highly prized by mushroom hunters. Touch it—what does it feel like?

Morchella

Worm-eating warbler

This is an Important Bird Area with large nesting populations of perching birds, like the worm-eating warbler, a species of special conservation concern. Sit quietly for five minutes in the forest along the trail. Close your eyes and listen. Birds often have two different types of sounds—a song (complex and having to do with territory and mating) and a call (shorter, like an alarm). Can you hear the different sounds birds make as you listen?

Helmitheros vermivorum

Canadian yew

This evergreen shrub is sometimes called a ground hemlock. This species is rare in Indiana, but can be found in this park. Look for its bright red, berry-like cone called an aril. Birds love eating them—when they poop out the seeds, it helps make more yews.

Taxus canadensis

28

ROUND THE RAVINES AT FORT HARRISON

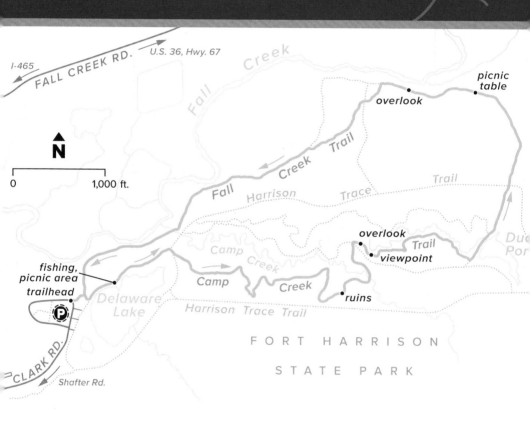

YOUR ADVENTURE

Adventurers, today you'll trek forests, ridgelines, and ravines on the historical homeland of the Miami. Prepare to cross creeks on this multi-trail loop through one of Indiana's newer state parks, formerly a military base. Fun fact— Lead Adventurer Sharon was stationed here in the early 1990s while enlisted in the US Navy. Today, Fort Harrison is an impressive park,

Immerse yourself in nature on this wooded path →

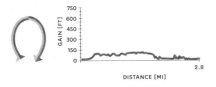

GAIN [FT]

750
600
450
300
150
0

2.8

DISTANCE [MI]

LENGTH 2.8-mile loop

ELEVATION GAIN 135 feet

DIFFICULTY Challenging—longer, rugged trail; can be a little difficult to navigate in parts

HIKE TIME + EXPLORE 2 hours

SEASON Year-round. Spring is ideal for woodland flowers.

GET THERE Head north on North Post Road in Indianapolis and turn left onto Shafter Road. Follow Shafter Road through the park entrance and continue straight to the first street, Clark Street, and turn right. Take that to the parking lot. The trailhead is near the walkway to Delaware Lake.

Google Maps: bit.ly/timbercampcreek

RESTROOM At trailhead

FEE $7 day fee for Indiana residents (annual passes available); $9 day fee for nonresidents

TREAT YOURSELF Get a sundae at Sundae's Homemade Ice Cream on 79th Street, about 4 miles from the park.

Fort Harrison State Park
(317) 591-0904
Facebook @FortBenIN
Facebook @FriendsofFortHarrison

containing four nature preserves. Take a loop connecting Camp Creek and Fall Creek Trails. Begin at Delaware Lake and follow Harrison Trace Trail along the shore. At the end of the lake, Harrison Trace Trail and Camp Creek Trail meet. Turn right and immediately look to the wooded area on the left. You'll see a well-worn, but not well-marked, trail. This is Camp Creek Trail. Take it up a short, steep ridge and follow the ridgeline. There are some unmarked trail intersections. Go left at the first one, at a sign about the nature preserve. At the next intersection, go left again. Camp Creek (CC) wayfinder signs and the creek below on the left show you're on the right path. Cross a stream and reach a bridge, and go left when the trail splits. Enjoy this immersion in nature. Pass a bridge and some old ruins from when this was a military base. Go straight at the junction to stay on Camp Creek, enjoying views of the creek below. Cross another stream and emerge at Duck Pond. Turn left and continue straight along the pond. Reach an intersection with Harrison Trace Trail. Continue straight across it through more woodland to an overlook, with Fall Creek below. Follow the creek and turn left onto Fall Creek Trail. Take this back and eventually intersect with the Harrison Trace Trail. Cut across it and follow Fall Creek Trail to emerge near the trailhead.

SCAVENGER HUNT

White-tailed deer

These mammals can be shy and elusive, but if you're quiet and look closely—and if you're on the trail in the early morning or late afternoon—you might spot one. If they see you, they might run. Deer can run 30 miles per hour! How fast can you run?

Odocoileus (means "hollow tooth" for the holes in their molars) *virginianus*

Bat house

Bat boxes provide safe places for bats to roost. There is one just north of Duck Pond. Can you find it? Fort Harrison is home to several bat species, including the little brown bat, big brown bat, and the state- and federally endangered Indiana bat. The box is high on a post in an open area, which is great for hunting insects. What other species like human-made homes?

The black paint-job on this box helps it absorb heat so the bat babies stay cozy

Lily pad

This plant lives in still water and looks like it's just a leaf floating, but it actually has a long stem that roots at the bottom of the water. There are water bodies along these trails, including a small slow-flowing creek, a large fast-flowing creek, and a pond. Where do you think you'll find water lilies?

Nymphaea odorata

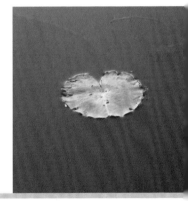

Blue wood aster

This perennial (blooms every year) wildflower abounds in the woods from spring to fall. If you find a fallen flower, press it between two pages in your nature journal and put something heavy on top of it overnight to make a flower press.

Symphyotrichum cordifolium

29

FOLLOW THE WHITE RIVER AT POTTER'S COVERED BRIDGE PARK

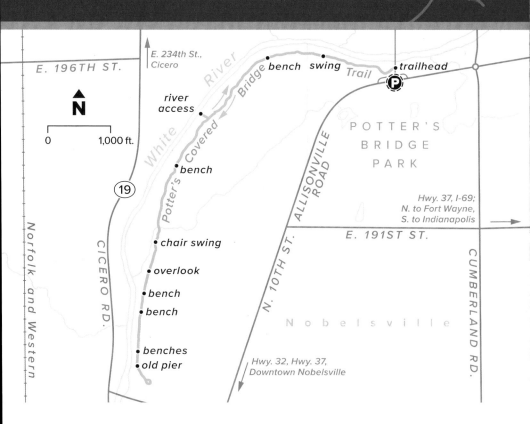

YOUR ADVENTURE

Adventurers, today you'll be exploring nature and history along the 362-mile-long White River on the historical homeland of the Miami. Begin your trek at the historical covered bridge—the last remaining original covered bridge in Hamilton County. Not far from the trailhead, you'll come to a covered swing inviting you to sit, relax, and enjoy the views of the White River. The

Fall is peak season for this trail →

GAIN [FT]

750
600
450
300
150
0

3.2

DISTANCE [MI]

LENGTH 3.2-mile out and back

ELEVATION GAIN 30 feet

HIKE TIME + EXPLORE 2 hours

DIFFICULTY Easy—flat, paved path with many benches

SEASON Year-round, but fall is spectacular for colorful foliage.

GET THERE In Noblesville, take 10th Street north to where it becomes Allison-ville Road. Potter's Bridge Park will be on your left in about a half mile. The trailhead begins at the covered bridge.

Google Maps: bit.ly/timbercoveredbridge

RESTROOM At trailhead

FEE None

TREAT YOURSELF Get lunch and hand-dipped ice cream at Alexander's on the Square on Logan Street, about 2 miles away in Noblesville.

Potter's Bridge Park
(317) 770-4400
Facebook @myhcpr

trail, which is part of the White River Greenway Trails System, follows the river's edge and is nicely shaded with maples, sycamore, and oak trees. This greenbelt serves as a wildlife corridor bridging a fragmented landscape so wildlife like beaver, waterfowl, and other animals can move through. You'll soon pass a bench and then come upon a little offshoot path down to the river's edge. Take a moment to sit by the river, listen, and watch nature around you. Many species come through this corridor. Next, you'll pass a bench, chair swing, another two benches, and some overlooks—rest and power up as needed. At the sign explaining the old piers, look closely for remnants of an old trolley system that was located on this spot over one hundred years ago, helping people commute from city to city. Turn around here and head back the way you came. Consider exploring more of the region by staying at the nearby White River Campground.

SCAVENGER HUNT

Northern harrier

This distinctive hawk looks like an owl but only hunts during the day. Unlike other hawks who use sight, harriers use sound to catch their prey. They soar low over the ground, searching for small mammals, reptiles, amphibians, and insects.

Circus hudsonius (*harrier* means "to harass" in Old English)

Painted rocks

Look closely along the trail and at the bases of trees—can you find any of the park's special painted rocks? If you find a flat river stone, you can make your own painted insect rock for your garden or planter.

Whimsical painted stones

Potter's covered bridge

This is the last covered bridge in Hamilton County. Covered bridges used to be prevalent across the country, but slowly were replaced by iron. Today, less than six hundred remain in the United States, and over ninety of them are in Indiana. Walk inside the bridge and take a picture of the sign about trusses. When you get home, try to build a bridge using popsicle sticks in one of the truss styles.

Howe truss bridge, erected in 1870

Post oak

The leaves of the post oak have a distinctive cross shape. Their scientific name, *stellata*, is the Latin word for "star." It refers to star-shaped hairs on the lower surface of the leaves. They are commonly called post oak because the timber is used to make fence posts. Find a fallen leaf and do a leaf rubbing in your nature journal.

Quercus stellata

Seasonal special: velvet shank

These bright orange-and-brown mushrooms arrive in late fall and early winter, usually on dead or dying oak, elm, or ash trees. Their scientific name, *flammulina*, refers to "little flames" for their color, while *velutipes* means "with velvet legs." Touch this mushroom gently. Do you think it feels like velvet?

Flammulina velutipes

EXPLORE EARTHWORKS AT MOUNDS STATE PARK

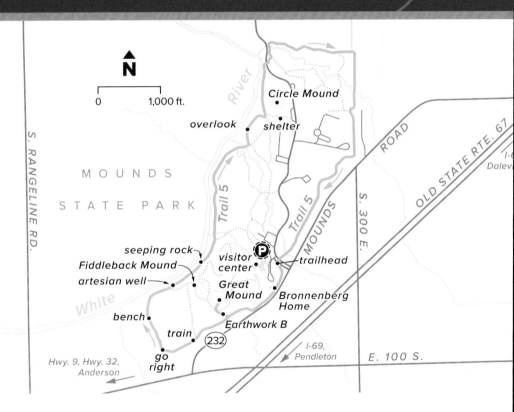

YOUR ADVENTURE

Adventurers, today you'll explore nature, culture, and history at Mounds State Park, on the historical homeland of the Adena-Hopewell. From the visitor center, head right on Trail 5 to the historical Bronnenberg House. This pioneer family protected the ancient Adena-Hopewell peoples' sacred earthworks from vandals and artifact hunters in the 1800s. Thanks to their

Explore nature, history, and culture →

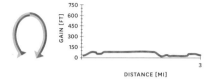

GAIN [FT]

750
600
450
300
150
0

DISTANCE [MI]

3

LENGTH 3-mile loop

ELEVATION GAIN 144 feet

HIKE TIME + EXPLORE 2 hours

DIFFICULTY Moderate—longer, with some steep inclines and rugged terrain

SEASON Year-round. Enjoy an abundance of flowers in spring or colorful leaves in fall.

GET THERE From IN-9 in Anderson, turn east onto Mounds Road for 1.5 miles, bear left onto IN-232, and turn left into the parking lot toward the visitor center. Park in the lot and pick up Trail 5 in front of the Historic Bronnenberg House, located on the south end of the visitor center parking lot.

Google Maps: bit.ly/timbermounds

RESTROOM At visitor center (if after hours, access on north side of building)

FEE $7 day fee for Indiana residents (annual passes available); $9 day fee for nonresidents

TREAT YOURSELF Grab lunch or a sweet treat at Sweet Paradise, about 5 miles south in Anderson.

Mounds State Park
(765) 642-6627
Facebook @moundsstatepark

efforts, this is the best-preserved site of the Adena-Hopewell culture in the state. Find an open grassy area with multiple small hills. These are the ancient mounds, dating as far back as 2000 years. Go right to see the Great Mound, the largest of the park's earthworks. Continue into the forest to learn the park's modern history. From 1897 to 1929 this was an amusement park. The path you're walking on was a railroad track. The trail leads to the White River, curves right, and goes along the waterfront. Find more historical remnants and unique geologic features like seeps and springs. Eventually, reach a steep climb to overlook the river, then cross a road. At an intersection, go left then right at the next trail junction. Pass the trail to the campground on the left. Turn right and follow the trail to a grassy area near the visitor center. Make a weekend of it and stay at the family campground at Mounds State Park.

SCAVENGER HUNT

Pileated woodpecker

This is the largest woodpecker species in Indiana. You can't miss them with that shock of bright red on their head. They also have a loud and distinctive call. Listen to it on the All About Birds website. Can you imitate their call?

Dryocopus (means "tree cleaver" in Latin) *pileatus* (means "crest" in Latin, for its mohawk)

Artesian well

It's hard to imagine, but the forest around you was cleared and used for an amusement park one hundred years ago! Only a few ruins remain. Can you find this concrete circular ruin that used to be a drinking fountain?

Remains from the past

Ancient mounds

Look closely and you'll notice small hills, called mounds, in an open area. There are ten of these historical earthworks here, created by the Adena-

Hopewell peoples as far back as 2000 years ago. Archaeologists (people who study ancient cultures) suggest the mounds were mostly used for ceremonial purposes, some having to do with stargazing. Lie down on the ground and look up at the sky—what do you think life was like 2000 years ago?

Sacred Adena-Hopewell earthworks

Black squirrel

These rodents (mammals with teeth that keep growing) are the same species as gray squirrels but have dark fur. It collects heat more than other colors, which means they stay warmer in winter. What kind of adaptation do you wish you had to live easier in your environment?

Sciurus carolinensis

Train station

Look down at the path and imagine you are walking on railroad tracks, because part of Trail 5 was a railbed one hundred years ago. Before most people had cars, trains are how they arrived here. See if you can find what remains of the old train stop.

All that remains from a historical train stop; Historical photo from Mounds State Park Archives

31

REMEMBER THE LOST SISTER AT MISSISSINEWA LAKE

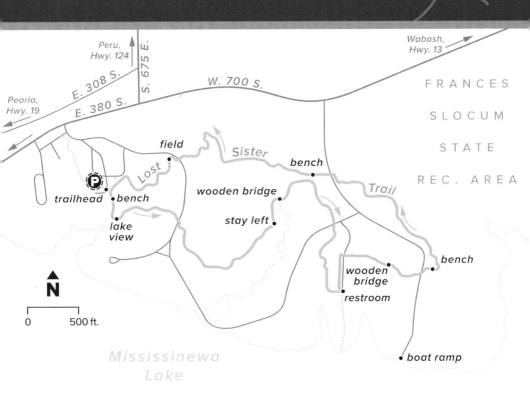

YOUR ADVENTURE

Adventurers, today you'll be exploring Lost Sister trail, named for Frances Slocum, who is also called Maconaquah, from the Miami language meaning "Little Bear Woman," because of her strength. Kidnapped by Delaware warriors as a child during the American Revolutionary War, she eventually married a Miami chief and settled in this area. She was reunited with her

This trail explores the 3180-acre Mississinewa Lake, which means "water on slope" in the Miami language →

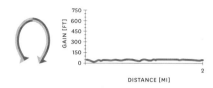

GAIN [FT]

750
600
450
300
150
0

DISTANCE [MI]

2

LENGTH 2-mile loop

ELEVATION GAIN 72 feet

HIKE TIME + EXPLORE 1.5 hours

DIFFICULTY Moderate—clearly marked trail with stairs

SEASON Year-round. Summer is a great time to cool off at the lake after your hike.

GET THERE From Peru, take IN-19 south to E 400 S. Head east for 2.9 miles. Turn left onto S 550 E then take an immediate right onto Mississinewa Dam Road. Go 0.8 miles, continuing onto E 380 S for 0.6 miles. Turn right into the parking lot and continue, with a slight right, through the lot to the trailhead.

Google Maps: bit.ly/timberlostsister

RESTROOM At trailhead

FEE None

TREAT YOURSELF Get a decadent dip at Southside Scoops, across the Mississinewa Dam on IN-19 S.

Mississinewa Lake State Park
(765) 473-6528
Facebook @mississinewa

siblings sixty years after her abduction. This trail is a tribute to her and this area, the historical homeland of the Miami. There is a monument at her gravesite nearby. As you meander through the woods, try to imagine what life might have been like along the Mississinewa River hundreds of years ago. Take the first right to begin the loop, and pass a lake view on the right. Continue through the woods and stay left at the fork just before Marker 14. You'll cross a small footbridge over a stream and then come to a road. Cross it and continue on the trail. About halfway along the loop, you'll reach a wide grassy open area with a shelter, near the edge of Mississinewa Lake. Consider stopping here for a picnic on the waterfront before continuing through the wooded forest along the trail. You'll come to another small bridge over a stream, then cross a parking lot and pass a boat ramp and bench. Make two more road crossings. The shady wooded trail will open up to a grassy picnic area before winding back through the woods to the trailhead. Consider staying for the weekend at nearby Mississinewa Lake Campground.

SCAVENGER HUNT

Yellow poplar

This is the tallest deciduous tree in North America. It usually has perfectly straight trunks, which were popular for carving out canoes. Its leaves are unique, with four lobes separated by rounded notches. Trace the notches in your nature journal.

Liriodendron tulipifera

Virginia wild rye

This native grass grows three feet tall. Size yourself up— are you taller than this grass? Follow the length of it to its seedhead at the top. Look even closer. Can you spot the spikelets that have florets on them? This is how the grass reproduces.

Elymus virginicus

Honey locust tree

Can you find long slender seed pods from this sweet deciduous (loses its leaves) tree? Its feathery leaves turn bright yellow in fall. Despite its name, it doesn't help make honey, but the white flowers in spring have a sweet smell and a taste that local wildlife love.

Gleditsia triacanthos

Snakeroot

This plant is named for a snake, but doesn't look like one. It may be named snakeroot because pioneers believed the roots could help treat snakebites. Feel its serrated (jagged-edge) leaves, and in spring, look for its umbel of white flowers, called such because they jut out from the center like the underside of an umbrella.

Sanicula ("healthy" in Latin because it's used for medical remedies) *odorata*

Baltimore oriole

Mississinewa Lake and the surrounding forests attract many bird species, like this bright orange-and-black songbird. Look in the tree canopy and foliage. Do you see any flashes of color? Their songs sound like a beautiful flute signaling springtime. Can you whistle? Try to make your own whistle song celebrating the season you're currently in.

Icterus galbula

32

PUCKER UP AT KISSING FALLS IN KOKIWANEE NATURE PRESERVE

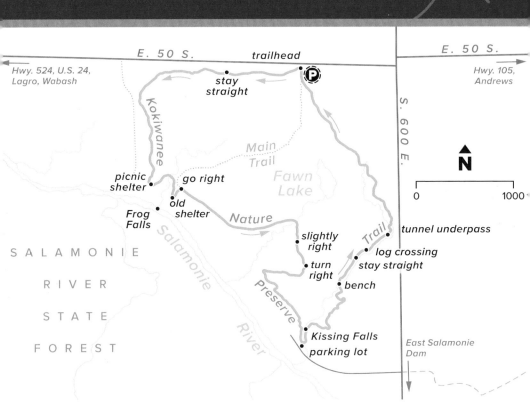

E. 50 S.   trailhead   E. 50 S.

Hwy. 524, U.S. 24, Lagro, Wabash

Hwy. 105, Andrews

stay straight

Kokiwanee

Main Trail

Fawn Lake

S. 600 E.

N

0   1000

picnic shelter

go right

old shelter

Frog Falls

Salamonie

Nature

slightly right

Trail

tunnel underpass

log crossing
stay straight

turn right

bench

SALAMONIE

RIVER

STATE

FOREST

Preserve

River

Kissing Falls
parking lot

East Salamonie Dam

YOUR ADVENTURE

Adventurers, today you'll visit Kissing Falls and explore a forest on the historical homeland of the Peoria. It was cleared for agriculture and then eventually allowed to return to a natural state. Begin by taking the trail to the right and walking through the woods. Stay straight and follow the path as it curves toward the 84.4-mile-long Salamonie River. Reach a picnic

20-foot-tall Kissing Falls is a highlight of this hike →

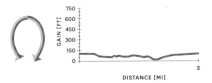

LENGTH 2-mile loop

ELEVATION GAIN 118 feet

HIKE TIME + EXPLORE 1.5 hours

DIFFICULTY Challenging—steep, rugged terrain on some parts of the trail

SEASON Year-round. Early spring has wildflowers, the most active waterfalls, and the chance to spot bald eagles.

GET THERE From IN-9 / Marion Road in Huntington, turn right on W Division Road and follow it for 7.6 miles. Turn left on S 600 E / County Road 600 E / Stone Road for 0.5 miles, then turn right on E 50 S for 0.2 miles. The parking lot for Kokiwanee is on the left.

Google Maps: bit.ly/timberkokiwanee

RESTROOM At gas station about 3 miles west of trailhead

FEE None

TREAT YOURSELF Get a cone at the Ice Cream Vault, about 7 miles northeast of the trail in Andrews.

Kokiwanee/ACRES Land Trust
(260) 637-2273
Facebook @ACRES.LT

shelter with a small opening in the forest, with sun-loving wildflowers and a great overlook. Follow the trail behind the shelter to an older shelter from when this was a Girl Scout camp. Go right at the fork, passing a trail on your left. Stay straight, then go right to the waterfall. It is very steep with loose rocks, so use caution. Pass a parking lot and at the bottom, you'll find Kissing Falls. This is a great place to play, power up, and look for wildlife along the streambed. Continue to the right of the waterfall on a short, steep incline, then reach a bench and bridge over a small stream. Stay straight at the intersection, following the stream to the underpass, which is sure to spark exploration. Follow the trail to the left to an open grassy pathway. Turn right and you're back at the parking lot. Consider camping nearby at Salamonie River State Forest Family Campground.

SCAVENGER HUNT

Linden tree

These deciduous trees (loses its leaves) are also called beetree linden because of the bounty of perfumed flowers they produce, which provide nectar for bees to make a delicious honey. See if you can find the linden tree that seems to be sprouting six trunks.

Tilia americana

Slender false foxglove

These plants produce 20–80 purple-pink flowers on a long spike from June to September and are a favorite flower for bumblebees. The name *foxglove* describes the shape of the flower, which some think looks like gloves with fingers that fit the paws of foxes. Sketch a fox wearing gloves in your nature journal.

Agalinis tenuifolia

Snow trillium

This rare plant isn't commonly found in Indiana, but it is on this trail in early spring, though it's tricky to spot. Stay on the trails when you're looking

for it. *Nivale* means "of snow" because it is one of the first flowers to bloom, often while snow is still on the ground. Look for its three (trillium) white petals and three green sepals (they kind of look like leaves and protect the petals). Can you count the six yellow stamens (pollen producers) in the middle?

Trillium nivale

Downy woodpecker

Listen for a tapping sound and try to spot this very small woodpecker. They are beneficial birds because they eat a lot of insects that can harm plants and crops. They are known to eat over forty types, including bark beetles, apple borers, and weevils. Can you name forty different kinds of foods you eat?

Dryobates pubescens

Dragonflies and damselflies

Look closely around the streambeds, waterfall, and river—while staying on the trail—and you might spot dragonflies and damselflies. These insects have two sets of wings that let them move like a helicopter. Damselflies are a bit smaller. Flap your arms and pretend to be a dragonfly.

Try to spot both a gray petaltail dragonfly (*Tachopteryx thoreyi*) and a blue-fronted dancer damselfly (*Argia apicalis*)

33

BOARDWALK AND REFLECT AT LINDENWOOD NATURE PRESERVE

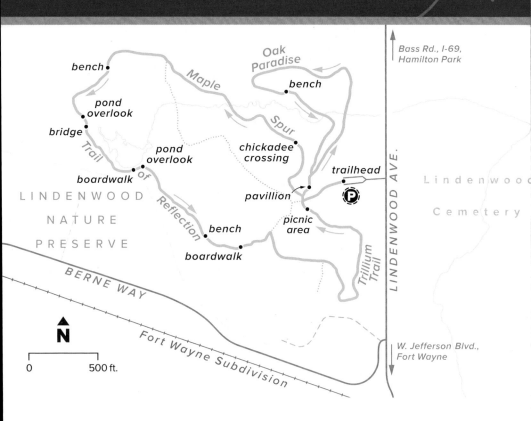

bench

pond overlook

bridge

boardwalk

LINDENWOOD

NATURE

PRESERVE

BERNE WAY

Oak Paradise

Maple

Spur

pond overlook

chickadee crossing

bench

boardwalk

pavillion

picnic area

trailhead

bench

Trail of Reflection

Trillium Trail

Fort Wayne Subdivision

Bass Rd., I-69, Hamilton Park

LINDENWOOD AVE.

Lindenwood Cemetery

W. Jefferson Blvd., Fort Wayne

N

0   500 ft.

YOUR ADVENTURE

Adventurers, today you'll escape into nature along a network of short trails on the historical homeland of the Peoria. Walk straight along the Path of Reflection Trail to the picnic benches and fire pit, which is a connection point for multiple trails. Go right before you reach the bird feeders, and follow the Oak Paradise Trail. It splits—go right, passing a bridge over a small

The pond provides a place for reflection →

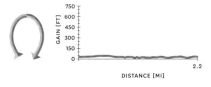

GAIN [FT]

750
600
450
300
150
0

2.2

DISTANCE [MI]

LENGTH 2.2-mile loop

ELEVATION GAIN 75 feet

HIKE TIME + EXPLORE 1.5 hours

DIFFICULTY Easy—well shaded and well-marked paths

SEASON Year-round. Good place to go in winter for the park's stargazing events.

GET THERE In Fort Wayne, head west on Jefferson Blvd to turn right on Lindenwood Ave. The Lindenwood Nature Preserve will be on the left. Park in the lot, and you'll see the trailhead.

Google Maps: bit.ly/timberlindenwood

RESTROOM At entrance

FEE None

TREAT YOURSELF Get an artistic treat at Sweet Monster Ice Cream, about 6 miles north on Lima Road.

Lindenwood Nature Preserve
(260) 427-6740
Facebook @LindenwoodNaturePreserve

stream. Loop around to a bench, and cross that same stream again, returning to the junction you started at. This is a great place to listen for woodpeckers and try to spot owls. Pass the pavilion and turn right onto the Maple Spur Trail, through a maple grove. Pass a bridge and reach a junction at the Trail of Reflection. Stay straight past the bench toward the 2-acre pond. There are multiple benches to power up and quietly observe nature. A boardwalk overlooks the pond, a nice place to watch for birds. Continue along the path, past a bench and boardwalk, to the connection point for the Trillium Trail. Turn right and look at the forest floor; it is carpeted in three species of trillium and other wildflowers during spring and summer. The path returns to the main picnic area and pavilion. Turn right to head back to the entrance.

SCAVENGER HUNT

Raccoon

These mammals are pretty handy. The English word *raccoon* comes from the Powhatan word *aroughcun,* which means "animal that scratches with its hands." Every summer for the past few years, a raccoon and her kits (babies) have been spotted near the pond and around the last bridge of Trail of Reflection.

Procyon lotor

Great horned owl

This raptor (bird that catches live prey) gets its name because of the two tufts on its head that look like horns. Their call sounds like "hoo hoohoooooo hoohoo." Imitate their call and see if they return it. This owl can sometimes be seen and heard on the Trail of Reflection and Maple Spur Trail.

Bubo virginianus

Wild ginger

Look for the heart-shaped leaves of this plant that tricks flies into pollinating it. In early spring, it has brownish-purple blooms. The flowers lay horizontally on the ground to attract flies emerging from the ground after winter. They mistakenly think the flowers are their favorite food (dead animals!).

They enter the flower to eat it, and pollen attaches to them as they travel from plant to plant. Why do you think flies mistake this flower for a dead animal?

Asarum canadense

Trillium

Visit in early spring to see wildflowers along the Trillium Trail. Their eye-catching flowers have different colors, but they all have something in common: three petals and three sepals (small petals that cover the bud). By summer, they're gone. Draw these beauties in your nature journal.

Trillium (means "three" in Latin) *grandiflorum*

Sugar maple

Have you ever eaten pancakes with maple syrup? You can thank this tree! The sweet sap from these deciduous (loses its leaves) trees is where pure maple syrup comes from. Sap is essentially the tree's blood, but don't worry, tapping it for syrup doesn't hurt the tree. They can live three hundred years. They attract many types of birds and mammals that also enjoy the sap.

Acer saccharum (means "sugar" in Latin)

34

TAKE DIANA'S CHALLENGE AT INDIANA DUNES NATIONAL PARK

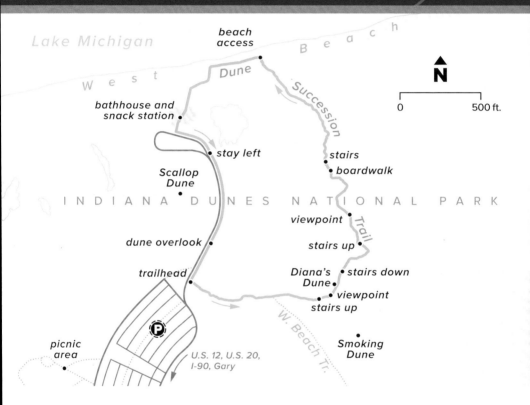

YOUR ADVENTURE

Adventurers, you're about to dune walk on the historical homeland of the Peoria. Start counterclockwise at Trailhead 2 on the West Beach Dune Succession Trail. You'll begin in sand and then quickly go up a boardwalk and staircase. Can you count how many stairs? At the top, look around you 36 miles out—can you spy Chicago? The boardwalk continues as you pass

Climb the stairs to paradise →

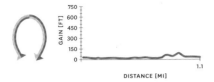

GAIN [FT]

750
600
450
300
150
0

DISTANCE [MI]

1.1

LENGTH 1.1-mile loop

ELEVATION GAIN 100 feet

HIKE TIME + EXPLORE 1.5 hours

DIFFICULTY Moderate—wonderfully short, but little legs on sand and stairs can make for slower going

SEASON Year-round. Spring has wildflowers and fewer crowds; great in summer to cool off.

GET THERE From Gary, follow US-12 / US-20 east to turn left onto County Line Road. Bear right onto W Beach Road / Main Street until the road ends at the West Beach parking lot.

Google Maps: bit.ly/timberindianadunes

RESTROOM At parking lot

FEE $5, payable by cash, check, or credit card

TREAT YOURSELF Head 7 miles south to Marilyn's Bakery in Hobart to try their famous Indiana sugar cream pie.

Indiana Dunes National Park
(219) 395-1882
Facebook @IndianaDunesNPS

Diana's Dune. Her name was actually Alice Mabel Gray, and she lived in the dunes from 1916 to 1918. Reporters nicknamed her Diana, after the goddess of the hunt. Be sure to take a selfie and post it online with #DianesDunesDare and collect a sticker at the visitor center for completing the dare. Continue going up and down the staircases throughout the dunes, and finally come out on West Beach. Turn left and walk toward the beach entrance, and then take the paved path through the bathhouse and back to the parking lot. Consider making it a very dune-y weekend and camp at Dunewood Campground just up the road.

SCAVENGER HUNT

Jack pine

This evergreen (doesn't lose its leaves) tree is a bit scraggly-looking and thrives in poor soils like sand, so it's a perfect inhabitant of the dunes. Isn't it wonderful how different plants prefer different environments, which means we can enjoy plants all over the world? Touch its pointy needles and look for its small cones, which can stay on the branches and not open for years. Is the cone you find today open (ready to let seeds out) or closed?

Pinus banksiana

Seasonal special: hoary vervain

This park has over 1000 native plants, like this showy flower that loves sandy soil and thrives here. Named for its hairy stem and leaves, it has a stalk of small, purple, nectar-filled flowers that insects love. How many flowers can you count on one stalk?

Verbena stricta

Sweet sumac

If you find a leaf on the ground near this decid-uous (loses its leaves) shrub, crush it in your hand and take a whiff. Does it smell sweet to you? It flowers in spring and then sprouts hairy red drupes as its fruit. Drupes look similar to berries, but they have only one seed, while berries have multiple seeds.

Rhus aromatica

Common hoptree

This deciduous (loses its leaves) shrub dots the dune landscape—can you count the three leaves on each stem? Look for its clusters of white flow-ers in spring, and then its fruit, which looks like a little package hanging down. It's called a samara and has little "wings" to help it disperse itself to grow more hop trees. If you find a samara on the ground, pick it up and twirl it to the ground—see if you can get it further than your hike mate's.

Ptelea trifoliata ("three leaves" in Latin)

Blue jay

Did you know that these song birds aren't actu-ally blue? They are brownish-grey, but when the light scatters on their feathers, they appear to be a magical blue. They migrate south, stop-ping along the Great Lakes in their search for a warmer climate. Do you like to go somewhere warm during winter?

Cyanocitta (*cyan* means "blue" in Latin) *cristata*

ADVENTURES IN
OHIO

Adventurers, heading east, you'll enter Ohio, a state born in 1803, named after the Seneca word for "great river," and nicknamed the Buckeye State for its distinctive state tree. Begin in Northern Ohio around Lake Erie, exploring the remnants of what was once the Great Black Swamp and today is dominated by farmland. Ferry over to Kelleys Island to see the most famous glacial grooves in the world, then continue east toward Cuyahoga Valley, a historical trade route for many Native American peoples, featuring hardwood forests, prairies, waterfalls, beautiful sandstone bluffs, and remarkable Sharon Conglomerate ledges. You'll experience pioneering history on a gorge trail that features a working mill and covered bridge from the 1800s. Then journey south toward the Hocking Hills, where caves, gorges, and waterfalls delight. See mysterious healing waters in Yellow Springs, explore creeks, cross a swinging bridge, and chase waterfalls in parks around Dayton before continuing south toward Cincinnati. There you'll trek a gorge, flex on a fitness trail, and hike Bender Mountain for an epic overlook of the Ohio River. Finally, witness an awesome earthwork effigy at Serpent Mound. Are you ready? Let's hit it!

35

STROLL THE BOARDWALK AT MAUMEE BAY

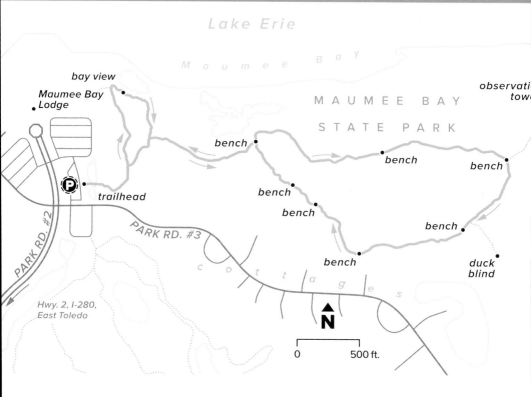

Lake Erie

Maumee Bay

MAUMEE BAY

STATE PARK

bay view

Maumee Bay
Lodge

observation
tower

bench

bench

bench

bench

trailhead

bench

bench

bench

PARK RD. #2

PARK RD. #3

bench

duck
blind

Hwy. 2, I-280,
East Toledo

cottages

N

0   500 ft.

YOUR ADVENTURE

Adventurers, today you'll explore a wetland on the historical homeland of the Peoria. This rich watery landscape is valuable and rare. Wetlands are one of the most endangered habitats in America. Almost all have vanished from Ohio, except here. Do you know the difference between a swamp, marsh, and bog? Begin at the Trautman Nature Center to find out. Then

Look down and around—animals abound! →

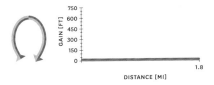

GAIN [FT]

750
600
450
300
150
0

1.8

DISTANCE [MI]

LENGTH 1.8-mile loop

ELEVATION GAIN 7 feet

HIKE TIME + EXPLORE 1–1.5 hours

DIFFICULTY Easy—flat walk along a boardwalk

SEASON Year-round. Late spring is spectacular for bird-watching, when an influx of bird migrants pass through, including thirty-six species of warbler. There is little shade on the boardwalk so wear sun protection and bug spray in summer.

GET THERE Head east through Oregon on Cedar Point Road to turn left on N Curtice Road. Follow it for a half mile and turn right onto Park Road 3; the Trautman Nature Center at Maumee Bay will be on your left. Park in the lot. The boardwalk trail begins behind the nature center.

Google Maps: bit.ly/timbermaumeebay

RESTROOM At trailhead

FEE None

TREAT YOURSELF Grab an ice cream next door at the Maumee Bay Lodge.

Maumee Bay State Park
(419) 836-9117
Facebook @MaumeeBayStatePark

start your nature exploration. Walk through a swamp forest with oaks, then stay left through the first junction and loop around to a bench overlooking Maumee Bay. When you reach a junction, turn left. As you stroll the boardwalk, look in the bright green duckweed covering the water. If you are patient, you'll likely begin to see animals like frogs, snakes, and turtles. They are carefully camouflaged (meaning they blend in). Hundreds of plant and animal species live or pass through here. Reach another junction at a bench—power up and stay left, passing another bench and arriving at another junction. Turn left and take the short offshoot to the duck blind to spot birds, then continue on the trail. Stay straight at the next junction. Walk by two more benches and arrive back at the original junction. Stay left here and at the next one to return to the trailhead. Consider adding to the adventure with a short half-mile stroll along the Storybook Trail, designed for families with young kids, that combines a love of nature and literature. Consider staying the weekend at the Maumee Bay Lodge.

SCAVENGER HUNT

Muskrat

These semi-aquatic rodents are very important for wetlands. They are smaller than beavers but larger than rats, and have dense fur. They make lodges and can stay underwater for about fifteen minutes at a time. How long can you hold your breath?

Ondatra zibethicus (means "musky in odor" in Latin)

Turtle

Look closely at logs and rocks. On sunny days you'll probably spot these reptiles (scaled and cold-blooded animals) sunning themselves. This marsh is home to several species, from common midland painted turtles to the very rare Blanding's turtle.

Chrysemys picta marginata

Water snake

These nonvenomous reptiles can often be seen lying on leaves and vegetation floating on the water. They are cold-blooded, meaning their body isn't naturally warm like ours, and they use water vegetation as a perch to warm up in the sun. How do you stay warm?

Nerodia sipedon

Button bush

This wetland shrub is named for its round blossoming seed heads, which have been described as tiny pincushions. Bumblebees and butterflies love this plant. It's also a favorite of muskrats, deer, dabbling ducks, and more. Give a button a soft poke—does it feel like a pincushion or just look like one?

Cephalanthus occidentalis

Great blue heron

When these large, tall birds are hunting for food, they wade slowly and stay as still as a statue before they strike. Do you know of any other animals that stalk their prey like that? Stay as still as a statue and scare your hiking buddy as they come around the corner on the trail!

Ardea herodias

36

GET GROOVY ON KELLEYS ISLAND

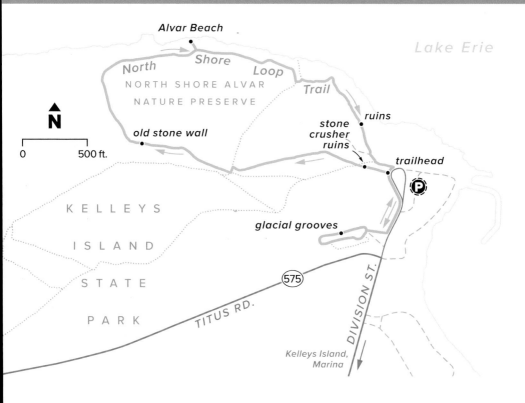

YOUR ADVENTURE

Adventurers, today you'll explore an island with the most famous glacial grooves in the world, as well as historical ruins from a limestone factory. Begin by boat, on the historical homeland of the Miami, on a twenty-minute ferry ride across Lake Erie to Kelleys Island. Ride 2 miles from the marina to the Glacial Grooves Preserve by bike, car, or golf cart. Follow the path

Explore famous glacial features →

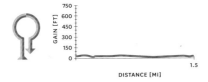

LENGTH 1.5-mile lollipop loop

ELEVATION GAIN 23 feet

HIKE TIME + EXPLORE 1 hour

DIFFICULTY Easy—short, flat walk

SEASON Year-round. Spring is recommended for wildflowers, and summer for beach and lake activities.

GET THERE Privately operated ferries offer daily service for vehicles, bicyclists, and pedestrians from the mainland at Marblehead. Or you can fly over via Griffing Airlines. Once you arrive on Kelleys Island, go left on E Lakeshore Drive for 0.5 miles. Turn right onto Division Street and follow it for 1.5 miles to the parking lot.

Google Maps: bit.ly/timberglacialgrooves

RESTROOM At public beach, across street from Glacial Grooves, just south of trailhead

FEE Ferry fees vary. No fee for the park.

TREAT YOURSELF Get a cone at Unc'l Dik's, a short walk from the trailhead.

Kelleys Island State Park
(419) 746-2546
Facebook @KelleysIslandStatePark

around the grooves, then head toward the road. Turn left and walk to the trailhead for the North Shore Loop. Stay left to start through a field of goldenrod, and see the huge Kelleys Island Lime and Transport Company stone crusher ruins on your right. Limestone was crushed here before being sent to lime kilns near the boat ramp. Stay right at the junction, and among the vegetation, spot an old stone wall on the left. These are remnants from a ramp that locomotives used to reach the crusher. Follow the trail to the right toward the shoreline. There is an offshoot path to a large, flat, rock beach called Alvar; power up and explore here. Look closely at the bedrock. Can you spot any fossils? Is there anything living in the small pools? Look for shorebirds and waterfowl. Continue along the trail to the stone crusher ruins, where tree canopies have replaced the roof as the walls slowly crumble away. Imagine what this looked like one hundred years ago. Follow the road back to the parking lot. Across the street is the public beach. Consider camping in Kelleys Island State Park and making a weekend of it.

SCAVENGER HUNT

Stone crusher

The main industry on Kelleys Island over one hundred years ago was quarrying limestone (which means removing it). It was used for many kinds of building materials, either in block form or crushed. This is an old stone crusher factory. Can you think of anywhere you have seen crushed stone used?

These lime kilns and crushers were built in the early 1900s; the original crusher closed around 1928 and today nature is reclaiming the ruins

Glacial grooves

This fenced and protected geologic marvel was made by nature 18,000 years ago when a mile-thick glacier cut huge grooves into the limestone bedrock. These are the best examples of glacial grooves in the world. Unfortunately, other glacial grooves on Kelleys Island were destroyed years ago. Draw these patterns in your nature journal.

The Megagroove

Ancient fossil

Lake Erie is freshwater, but 400 million years ago, this was a tropical saltwater sea. The bedrock of Kelleys Island was created by ancient animals who lived here millions of years ago. Today it has many fossil remains. Look closely at the bedrock along the shoreline and at the grooves. Can you find any fossils? What kind of marine creatures do you think lived here?

Marine life from the past

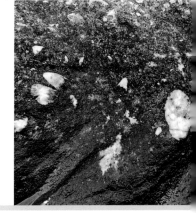

Seasonal special: lakeside daisy

This is one of few places to see this endangered plant, which is one of Ohio's most spectacular wildflowers. They bloom about the same time in April to May, and all the golden flower heads track the sun across the sky in unison. Draw this rare beauty in your nature journal, then check back on it in a few hours to see if it moved its head with the sun.

Tetraneuris herbacea is endangered

37

DISCOVER FOLK ART AT WORDEN'S LEDGES

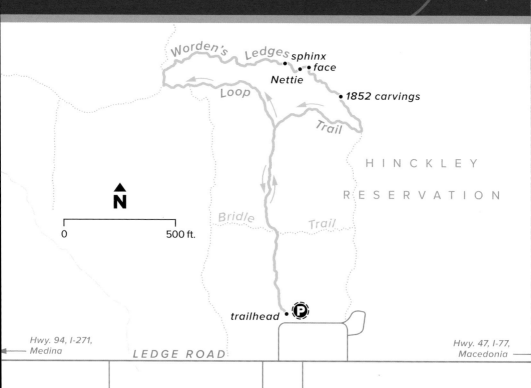

YOUR ADVENTURE

Adventurers, today you'll explore a trail that combines nature, folk art, and history. Meander through a forest along sandstone ledges on the historical homeland of the Erie. In the early 1900s, this was the homestead of Hiram Worden. His son-in-law, Noble Stuart, left a lasting artistic mark on the landscape in the mid-1940s by carving the faces of people and imagery

Sphinx guards the trail →

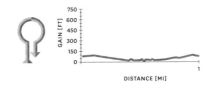

LENGTH 1-mile lollipop loop

ELEVATION GAIN 92 feet

HIKE TIME + EXPLORE 45 minutes–1 hour

DIFFICULTY Easy—short, well-shaded trail

SEASON Year-round, but fall is a great time for solid ground (the trail can get mucky) and cooler temperatures.

GET THERE Head south on on OH-94 through Hinckley to turn left on Ledge Road. The parking lot will be on your left in 1.4 miles.

Google Maps: bit.ly/timberwordens

RESTROOM At trailhead

FEE None

TREAT YOURSELF Indulge in delectable flavors of artisan ice cream at Chill in quaint, picturesque downtown Medina.

Worden's Ledges at Hinckley Reservation
(330) 278-2160
Facebook @ClevelandMetroparks

from his own life into the sandstone. Start down a dirt path into an open forest among hickory, oak, and maples. Stay on the path to protect the ferns, lichens, and mosses you'll see around you. Go left, following the raccoon trail blazes. Stay straight past the Bridle Trail, then go right on the Ledge Lake Loop Trail. Come to a guardian of the trail—a large carving of a sphinx. You're entering the folk-art zone, where Stuart lovingly carved the name of his wife, Nettie, along with faces, names, and dates memorializing his family's history, religious symbols, a ship, and other objects that had meaning to him. How many carvings can you find? At the end, turn right, back on the Worden's Ledge Loop Trail. Follow it to the beginning of the loop, then return to the parking lot. For fun, try exploring this trail at night using headlamps to follow the white racoon blazes.

SCAVENGER HUNT

Pirate ship

Pretend you're a pirate on a treasure hunt, and find your ship! It's not a real ship, but rather one that was carved into the soft conglomerate sandstone by Noble Stuart, a bricklayer and aspiring sculptor who carved imagery that inspired him. Think of something that inspires you, and draw it in your nature journal.

Schooner

Find the faces

Faces are the main carvings throughout the ledges. Look carefully to spot George Washington, Thomas Jefferson, Marquis de Lafayette (a French general), and Hiram Worden himself. How many faces can you find? Try to draw your lead hiker's face in your nature journal—is it easy or hard to draw people's faces?

Ty Cobb, a baseball player

Orange jewelweed

These flowers are a secret weapon against itchy poison ivy. If you accidentally touch poison ivy, mash up jewelweed and apply it to skin to reduce the itchiness—though soap and water is better. To avoid poison ivy, remember the rhyme: "leaves of three, leave it be."

Impatiens capensis

Web worm

Look in the trees and you might find something that looks like cotton candy. The white webbing of the fall webworm is hard to miss. This is a moth that lives in large groups of larvae and creates giant webs on the end of tree branches. Look closely at the web and you'll notice lots of little worms. How many can you count?

Hyphantria cunea makes fuzzy trees

American toad

These amphibians (live on water and land) help with insect control. Look around the forest floor and among the leaves and see if you can find one. They have thick skin with noticeable warts that are red or yellow. Don't touch! Their warty skin produces a poisonous fluid that protects them against predators. Hop along and imitate how the toad moves through the forest.

Anaxyrus americanus

38

LOOP THE LEDGES AT CUYAHOGA VALLEY NATIONAL PARK

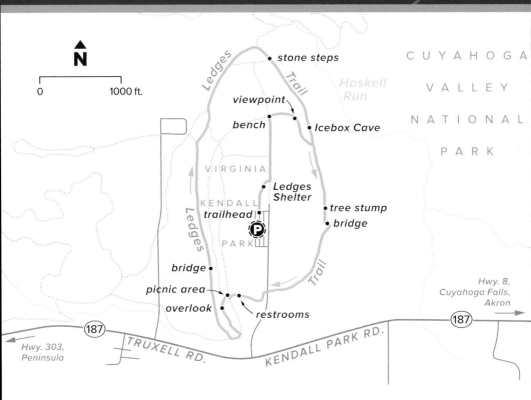

YOUR ADVENTURE

Adventurers, today you'll explore an ancient plateau of unique geological features, on the historical homeland of the Erie. Begin near Ledges Shelter, a historical building built by the Civilian Conservation Corp (CCC) in the 1930s. Shortly past the trailhead, reach a bench and interpretive panel about Ritchie's Ledges. Turn right and walk along the ledge. Make another

Remarkable rock formations and views along the trail →

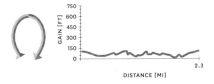

GAIN [FT] 750 600 450 300 150 0

DISTANCE [MI] 2.3

LENGTH 2.3-mile loop

ELEVATION GAIN 256 feet

HIKE TIME + EXPLORE 2 hours

DIFFICULTY Moderate—longer, with rugged and sometimes uneven terrain, stone stairs, and elevation

SEASON Year-round.

GET THERE Take I-80 to exit 180 and merge onto OH-8 South. In 2.2 miles, take Exit 12 for OH-303 and continue on Akron Cleveland Road to go right onto Kendall Park Road. In 1 mile, turn right toward Ledges Shelter parking lot.

Google Maps: bit.ly/timberledges

RESTROOM At trailhead

FEE None

TREAT YOURSELF Experience unique and decadent ice cream flavors at Country Maid Ice Cream & Orchard, located about 6 miles west on OH-303.

Cuyahoga Valley National Park
(440) 717-3890
Facebook @CuyahogaValleyNationalPark

right onto the Ledges Trail, which leads through a shaded forest featuring Eastern hemlocks, beech, and hickory. Cross a bridge and then a road. Then pass a picnic area, following the trail left to the Ledges Overlook with a view of the Cuyahoga Valley. The flat, bare rock ledges are a perfect viewing platform and place to power up and take in the scenery. Follow the trail to a fork and go right. This takes you down and around the ledge to appreciate the unusual rock formations, ferns, mosses, and other plant species that thrive in the cool, moist climate. There are crevices to explore along the ledges, as well as a bridge as you make your way to Ice Box Cave. Pass two trail connectors that provide shortened hike options, but keep straight. At the wayfinder sign for Ice Box Cave, go right. Pass stone stairs laid by the CCC—stay straight here—and reach Ice Box Cave. It is closed to protect bats that use the cave. Just past it, turn right and head back on the trail you came from, following it back to the parking lot. Consider camping nearby at the Ottawa Overlook backcountry sites.

SCAVENGER HUNT

Rock ledges

Try to imagine this place 315–320 million years ago. It was a fast-flowing delta riverbed. The rock ledges provide a window into the ancient past. Look, but do not climb! Life on the ledges is fragile. Carefully observe the different plants and animals clinging to the ledges. How many kinds can you find?

Sharon Sandstone and Conglomerate

White rot fungus

Watch for a crusty white fungus that looks like latex paint on fallen trees along the trail. White rot fungus is hungry and efficient and devours the most rigid, sturdy part of trees, called lignin. Scientists are just beginning to understand how valuable this fungus is for its carbon-drinking capabilities. How many differently shaped and colored fungi can you find?

Phanerochaetaceae

Beech tree

You'll immediately recognize the beech tree by its smooth gray bark. In ancient times, Germanic cultures used beech bark to inscribe books. The word *book* may have come from their word, *boko*, which means "beech." Sadly, some people inscribe on live beech trees. Never do this—it hurts the trees! Instead, imagine your favorite book written on pieces of bark.

Fagus grandifolia (*grandi* means "large" and *folia* means "leaf")

Big brown bat

There are seven species of bats in the park, including the big brown bat. You can't go into Ice Box Cave because it's closed for their protection, but you might spot them during the evening. Look for erratic flight patterns that are unlike birds. Bats see with sound—called echolocation. In the field area near Ledges Shelter, pretend to be a bat. Close your eyes and find your way for one minute using only sound. How did you do?

Eptesicus fuscus

39

WEND YOUR WAY TO BRANDYWINE FALLS

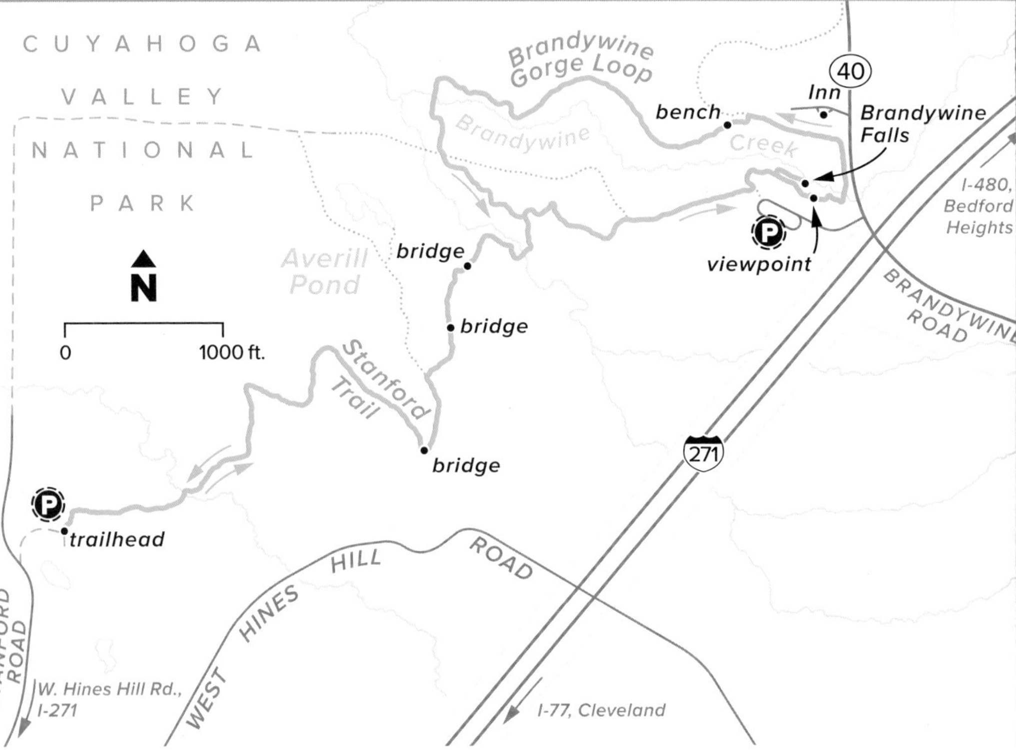

YOUR ADVENTURE

Adventurers, today you'll travel terrain that is sometimes steep and rugged on your way to Brandywine Falls, on the historical homeland of the Erie. Begin at Stanford House, named for James Stanford, one of the original settlers of the Western Reserve in 1805. The trail starts in open, sunny prairie, then winds into shaded forest with a steep incline. Cross a couple of bridges

Enjoy the views of the 60-foot falls →

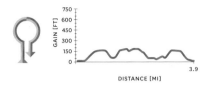

LENGTH 3.9-mile lollipop loop

ELEVATION GAIN 449 feet

HIKE TIME + EXPLORE 2–2.5 hours

DIFFICULTY Challenging—longer, with some steep, rugged terrain

SEASON Year-round. In spring, vernal pools along the Brandywine Gorge Trail temporarily fill with water, attracting breeding salamanders. In winter, the falls become an ice sculpture.

GET THERE Take Stanford Road north from Boston Mills Road for 0.5 miles. Make a right into the drive at Stanford House. There is a small parking lot behind the brown barn. If it is full, the next nearest lot is at the Boston Mill Visitor Center.

Google Maps: bit.ly/timberstanford

RESTROOM At Boston Mill Visitor Center and along the trail near Brandywine Falls.

FEE None

TREAT YOURSELF Enjoy frozen custard, a malt, or a banana split at Rosati's Frozen Custard, about 6 miles north on E Aurora Road.

Cuyahoga Valley National Park
(440) 546-5994
Facebook @CuyahogaValleyNationalPark

before reaching a trail connector for Averill Pond. Keep right, passing three more bridges. Descend steeply to a fork. Go right toward Brandywine Falls, taking steep stairs. Turn right and take the boardwalk and stairs to the lower falls overlook. There are cool rock ledges along the way, and a fantastic viewing area for Brandywine Falls. After you've rested, climb the stairs and turn left toward the upper falls viewing area, where you'll see ruins from the Champion Electric Company that was here one hundred years ago. Signs share the history of the area, which also had a gristmill. Turn left on the Bike and Hike Trail, crossing the falls and passing an open grassy area with picnic tables and the Inn at Brandywine Falls. Go left at the Brandywine Gorge Trail. There are offshoots along the trail, providing access to Brandywine Creek, a tributary of the 84.9-mile-long Cuyahoga River. Splash and explore in the shallow creek, or enjoy a power-up. Cross a bridge, trekking through forests with large oak trees before reaching the original fork in the trail. Turn right and return to Stanford House. Make a weekend of it and stay at the Stanford House or Inn at Brandywine Falls. Camping is offered nearby at Ottawa Overlook backcountry sites.

SCAVENGER HUNT

Ruins

Can you imagine Brandywine Village in 1814 as settlers lived right here where you walk? Brandywine Falls was harnessed for energy one hundred years ago, and ruins from a factory near the top of the waterfall remind us of this history. The cinder blocks represent the last industry in Brandywine Village. Did you know that water falling can create electricity? What are some other sources of energy?

Champion Electric Company ruins

Seasonal special: great blue lobelia

This plant, which blooms from July to September, is specially designed for bees. Look at the shape of the lower three petals—they create a landing pad for them. Each stem sprouts many flowers. How many can you count?

Lobelia siphilitica

Blue mud wasp

This beautiful shiny-colored insect is harmless and nonaggressive to people, but loves to feast on black widow spiders. It also pollinates many wildflowers. Draw it in your nature journal and see if you can make that dazzling blue color.

Chalybion californium

Northern spicebush

This shrub is covered in yellow flowers in spring and sprouts red berries in summer and fall. It is beneficial for people as a spice for food, as well as

medicine. It is also the host plant for spicebush swallowtails. The caterpillars of these large butterflies have unique markings, like a costume, that mimic the face of a snake to trick birds not to eat them. Pretend to be an animal and have your trail mate try to guess what you are.

Lindera benzoin

40

TREK TUNNELS AT NELSON KENNEDY LEDGES STATE PARK

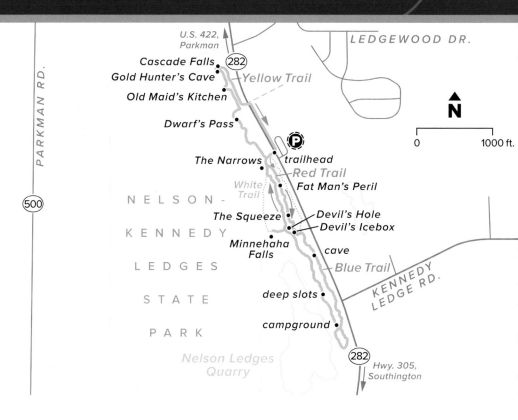

YOUR ADVENTURE

Adventurers, today you'll explore an otherworldly landscape so different from the surrounding area that it may feel like you're on another planet. Nelson Ledges is on the historical homeland of the Erie and Mississauga. Enter the forest through The Narrows, following the red trail blazes to the left through spectacular rock formations. These towering, jumbled

Transport yourself to this otherworldly landscape →

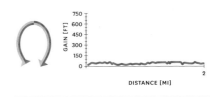

DISTANCE [MI]

LENGTH 2-mile loop

ELEVATION GAIN 148 feet

HIKE TIME + EXPLORE 1.5 hours

DIFFICULTY Challenging—rugged
terrain with some rock scrambling
and tight squeezes

SEASON Year-round. Winter is a beautiful
time to see the frozen waterfall; spring
delights with rare wildflowers.

GET THERE From Cleveland, take US-422
to OH-282 and turn south 1.7 miles to Nelson
Kennedy Ledges State Park. Turn left into
the parking lot. The trailhead is directly
across the street.

Google Maps: bit.ly/timbernelsonkennedy

RESTROOM At parking lot

FEE None

TREAT YOURSELF Get a malt
or sundae at Frozen Dee-lite Café
about 3 miles from the park.

Nelson Kennedy Ledges State Park
(330) 654-4989
Facebook @Ohiostateparks

slump blocks are called Sharon Conglomerate. It is 300 million years old, embedded with shiny white quartz pebbles, and covered in emerald-green mosses and ferns, with giant tree roots snaking down the sides. Climb down into the gorge and hike through a tight passageway called Fat Man's Peril before really getting tight at The Squeeze. Reach the deep, rocky cavern aptly named Devil's Hole. Continue through another narrow passage to a creek with a huge cave called Devil's Ice Box. The red trail ends here and the blue trail begins. Go right and walk along the creekbed, then cross a bridge and climb the stairs. Follow the trail along the sandstone ledge, passing a small cave and continuing through the woods. Curve to the right and spot the Nelson Ledges Quarry Park Campground to the left. Notice the deep crevices where the ground shifted and split ages ago. Cross a short bridge over a deep ravine and reach a junction with the white trail. To the left is Minnehaha Falls. Turn here to check it out, then return and go right. At the next junction, turn right and arrive back at The Narrows. Turn left and follow the white trail blaze north. Pass more unique rock formations with imaginative names like Dwarf's Pass, Old Maid's Kitchen, and Gold Hunter's Cave before reaching Cascade Falls. Turn right before the falls and aim for the trailhead. You'll exit just north of the parking lot; turn right to return to your car. Camping is offered nearby at Nelson Ledges Quarry Park Campground.

SCAVENGER HUNT

Coral fungus

This uniquely shaped fungus appears in late summer and fall. There are two hundred species of coral fungi, and they decompose dead things in the forest. Look closely—can you spot the branches? How many can you count? Look even closer—there are spores on each branch that help them reproduce.

Ramaria

Yellow birch

These deciduous (loses its leaves) trees seem to be growing straight out of the rocks. It is rare to find in Ohio, as it is

more common in the higher-elevation Appalachian Mountains. If you find a broken twig, sniff it. What does it smell like?

The roots of *Betula alleghaniensis* cling to the rocks

Tunnels and passageways

Exploring these tight squeezes is probably why you came. The passageways are unusual and different from other kinds of slot canyons because they are created from jumbled slump block. Notice the square, blocky formations. Rangers created fun names for them. Use your imagination— what would you name a tunnel here?

The Squeeze

Seasonal special: red trillium

This rare plant with blood-red petals grows on the ledges here in spring, yet is rarely found elsewhere in Ohio. It's beautiful, but smelly. Its nickname is Stinking Benjamin, and it attracts pollinators like flies and beetles, who like gross smells. Some people think it smells like a wet dog. What does it smell like to you?

Trillium erectum

41

CROSS THE COVERED BRIDGE AT MILL CREEK PARK

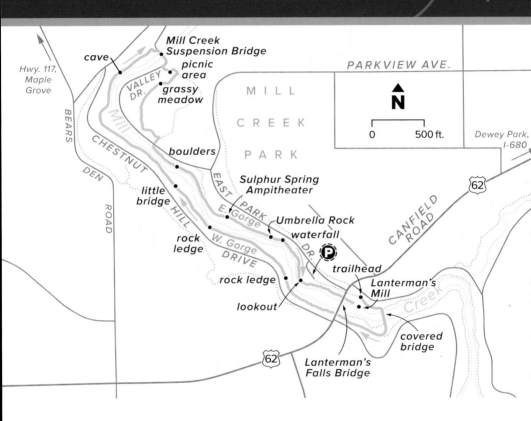

Hwy. 117, Maple Grove

cave

Mill Creek Suspension Bridge

picnic area

VALLEY DR.

grassy meadow

PARKVIEW AVE.

MILL

CREEK

PARK

N

0   500 ft.

Dewey Park, I-680

BEARS

Mill

CHESTNUT

boulders

62

DEN

ROAD

little bridge

EAST PARK

E. Gorge

HILL

W. Gorge

DRIVE

rock ledge

Sulphur Spring Ampitheater

Umbrella Rock

waterfall

DR.

CANFIELD ROAD

P

trailhead

rock ledge

lookout

Lanterman's Mill

Creek

covered bridge

62

Lanterman's Falls Bridge

YOUR ADVENTURE

Adventurers, today you'll learn a bit of history while exploring the oldest park district in Ohio, on the historical homeland of the Kaskaskia. Start at the historical Lanterman's Mill to see how a waterwheel powers 1500-pound stones to grind cornmeal and flour—the same way it was done in the 1800s. Then set off left on the Gorge Trail. Pass the pollinator

Lanterman's Mill was built in 1845 →

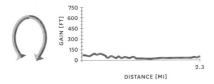

GAIN [FT]

DISTANCE [MI]

2.3

LENGTH 2.3-mile loop

ELEVATION GAIN 125 feet

HIKE TIME + EXPLORE 1.5–2 hours

DIFFICULTY Easy—mostly flat, well-shaded path

SEASON Year-round. Fall is lovely for the changing colors, while winter provides incredible ice formations in the gorge.

GET THERE Take Youngstown-Salem Road / US-62 south through Youngstown to E Park Drive and turn right. There is a small parking lot on the left and another one a little further along the road. Walk down to Lanterman's Mill. The trail begins behind the mill.

Google Maps: bit.ly/timbermillcreekgorge

RESTROOM At mill, when open (Tuesday–Sunday 10 a.m.–5 p.m. May–October)

FEE None

TREAT YOURSELF Have a creamy treat at Handel's Homemade Ice Cream, less than 2 miles away on Handel's Court.

Mill Creek Park
(330) 740-7115
Facebook @millcreekmetroparks

garden and restrooms, cross the covered bridge, and follow the paved road to the right. You'll see a sign for the West Gorge Trail on the right, at the top of the access road hill. Follow it underneath Lanterman's Falls Bridge and through the gorge, where you'll pass massive fern-covered rock walls and impressive rock ledges. Pass a bridge, a bench, and a cool little cave to explore before reaching one more bench. Cross the Mill Creek Suspension Bridge and the road, then turn right. Reach The Flats, a grassy picnic area with numerous benches to power up. At the far end, cross Valley Drive and enter East Gorge Walk. Follow it along the edge of Mill Creek, then reach a small area that looks like the remnants of a stone fountain. In the late 1800s, this was a sulfur spring that attracted people for miles around. Next, reach an elevated boardwalk and a waterfall at Umbrella Rock—a large rock overhang. Come to a lookout point for Lanterman's Falls. Go underneath the bridge and back to the mill where you started. This park offers many more trails—pick up a guide at the gift shop and consider your next adventure.

SCAVENGER HUNT

Bridges

This trail features several bridges with different architectural styles. Bridges were covered in the early to mid-1800s to protect the wood. By the

late 1800s, wrought and cast iron became cheaper and more available to replace wood. The Suspension Bridge, built in 1895, has fanciful features. It's been called many names, including Cinderella Bridge, Castle Bridge, and Silver Bridge. What would you call it?

Lanterman's Mill Covered Bridge

Pearl crescent butterfly

The pollinator garden near Lanterman's Mill is designed to attract monarch butterflies, and many wildflowers along the trail attract others, like this pearl crescent. Butterflies aren't just beautiful, they're beneficial. One out of every three bites of food you eat exists because of the work of pollinators. Name your favorite fruit and vegetable. Now thank butterflies (and bees, bats, and other pollinators) who make those foods available.

Phyciodes tharos

River otter

These are playful mammals—they love to wrestle, somersault, and slide on their bellies. Thanks to conservationists, river otter populations in Ohio

are rebounding from near extinction. They can be tricky to spot though, so watch closely and maybe you'll see one. They are excellent swimmers and spend about a third of their lives in the water. They are also very clean and wash themselves after every meal. Pretend to be a river otter and do a few somersaults.

Lontra canadensis

Vermilion waxcap

Can you find these colorful bright red gilled mushrooms along the trail? This is a cosmopolitan species, which means it can be found worldwide. Can you guess why it is called a waxcap? Give it a gentle touch. What does it feel like to you?

Hygrocybe miniata

42

VISIT OLD MAN'S CAVE IN HOCKING HILLS STATE PARK

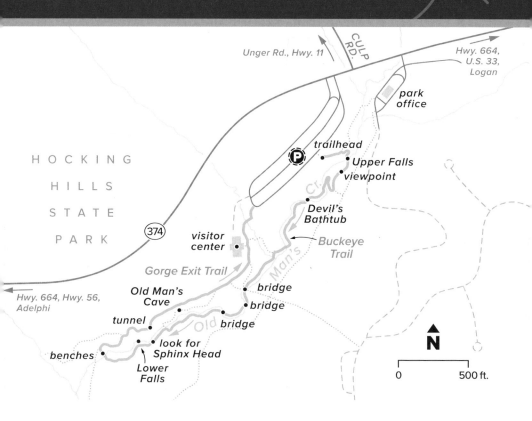

Unger Rd., Hwy. 11

CULP RD.

Hwy. 664, U.S. 33, Logan

park office

trailhead

Upper Falls viewpoint

HOCKING

HILLS

STATE

PARK

374

Cr.

Devil's Bathtub

visitor center

Buckeye Trail

Gorge Exit Trail

Man's

Hwy. 664, Hwy. 56, Adelphi

Old Man's Cave

bridge

bridge

tunnel

Old

bridge

benches

look for Sphinx Head

Lower Falls

N

0   500 ft.

YOUR ADVENTURE

Adventurers, today you'll explore one of Ohio's most magnificent parks, on the historical homelands of the Wyandot, Delaware, and Shawnee. The Grandma Gatewood trailhead begins at Upper Falls on the blue-blazed Buckeye Trail. This popular route is one-way to reduce congestion. You're immediately rewarded with views of the waterfall as you cross the stone

This gorge impresses around every bend →

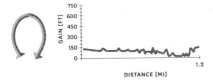

LENGTH 1.2-mile loop

ELEVATION GAIN 259 feet

HIKE TIME + EXPLORE 1.5 hours

DIFFICULTY Moderate—
stairs and some elevation

SEASON Year-round. Spring is recommended for wildflowers and fewer crowds.

GET THERE From Columbus, take US-33 to the OH-664 S exit toward Logan/Bremen.

Turn right and go 1.5 miles. Turn left to stay on OH-664 S and go 8.7 miles. Turn left into Hocking Hills State Park, and park at the visitor center. The Grandma Gatewood trailhead is near the north end of the parking lot.

Google Maps: bit.ly/timberhockinghills

RESTROOM At visitor center

FEE None

TREAT YOURSELF Grab snacks, ice cream, or other goodies at Old Man's Cave General Store, about 2.5 miles from the trailhead.

Hocking Hills State Park
(740) 385-6842
Facebook @Hockinghillsstatepark

bridge and head down into the gorge. At the bottom, power up and enjoy the views of Upper Falls, then continue. Cross a bridge and reach Devil's Bathtub, a swirling cascade that drops into a deep basin, creating a whirlpool. Cross the bridge and continue through the gorge, where hemlocks are plentiful. Ferns and lichen cling to the Black Hand Sandstone, which is 355 million years old. Cross five bridges to approach Old Man's Cave. Don't take the trail across the bridge toward the cave, though, because it leads to an exit and you still have more to see. Instead, continue straight to an observation point. Try to spot Sphinx Head across the creek. Walk beneath a rock ledge and behind a waterfall, then cross a bridge. There are benches here to power up before climbing the stone stairs through a tunnel, then turning right and exiting the gorge. Turn left and follow the path back toward the visitor center. Consider staying the weekend in the Hocking Hills State Park Lodge or campground.

SCAVENGER HUNT

Old Man's Cave

This geological feature is named after Richard Rowe, who lived in the cave beginning in 1796, and some say is still buried there. It's called a recess cave, and was carved by water. Could you live in a cave? What would it be like?

The cave is 200 feet long, 50 feet high, and 75 feet deep

Seasonal special: pink lady's slipper

This orchid reminds some people of a delicate fairy-sized slipper. Put your fingers behind them like legs and take a selfie of your finger shoes. Follow the stem down to the ground—this flower has its leaves at the bottom of the stem.

Cypripedium acaule

Upper and Lower Falls

This trail includes waterfalls along Old Man's Creek. It starts at Upper Falls and ends near Lower Falls, but there are more waterfalls along the path.

Upper Falls is a cascade, dropping onto several levels of rock, while Lower Falls is a plunge, because the water drops away from the cliff. Make a plunge waterfall from your water bottle into your mouth.

Start at Upper Falls (left) and end at 30-foot Lower Falls (right)

Devil's Bathtub

Bridges are abundant along this trail. This one is over Devil's Bathtub, a tiered cascade that swirls into a deep basin of water. The tub continues to get bigger and bigger as the water erodes the Black Hand Sandstone. Guess how many bridges you will cross, then count them along the way and see who comes closest to the right answer.

The whirlpool is only a few feet deep

Sphinx Head

This distinctive face oversees the plunge down to Lower Falls and is carved from rock that is 350 million years old. Look for signs of weathering on the cheeks of the sphinx—water slowly removed individual grains of sand to reveal this shape. Now look at its chin—that was caused by water from below taking off larger chunks of rock.

This stone formation is made of Black Hand Sandstone

43

RISE UP TO BUZZARD'S ROOST NATURE PRESERVE

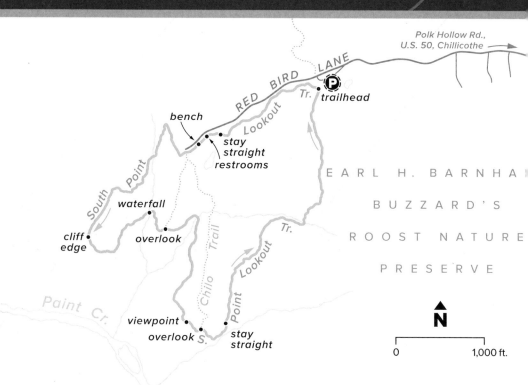

Polk Hollow Rd.,
U.S. 50, Chillicothe

RED BIRD LANE

Tr. trailhead

bench

Lookout

stay straight

restrooms

South Point

EARL H. BARNHA

BUZZARD'S

waterfall

cliff edge

overlook

Tr.

Chilo Trail

Lookout

ROOST NATURE

PRESERVE

N

Paint Cr.

viewpoint

overlook S.

Point

stay straight

0   1,000 ft.

YOUR ADVENTURE

Adventurers, today you'll explore the forest, cross creeks and waterfalls, and trek along the cliff edge. You'll see a spectacular view over Paint Creek Gorge and the foothills of Appalachia, on the historical homeland of the Miami. Start on South Point Lookout Trail, using the trailhead closest to the road, near the firepit. Follow the red trail blazes through woodlands.

View from South Point Trail →

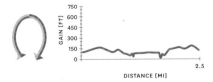

GAIN [FT]
750
600
450
300
150
0
2.5
DISTANCE [MI]

LENGTH 2.5-mile loop

ELEVATION GAIN 290 feet

HIKE TIME + EXPLORE 1.5–2 hours

DIFFICULTY Moderate—longer, with a bit of elevation and steep cliffs

SEASON Year-round. Wildlife viewing is at its peak in winter.

GET THERE From Chillicothe, take US-50 W / Western Avenue and turn left onto Polk Hollow Road. Follow 1.8 miles, take a sharp right onto Red Bird Lane, and go 0.8 miles to the parking lot of the South Point Lookout Trailhead.

Google Maps: bit.ly/timberbuzzardsroost

RESTROOM Yes, along trail

FEE None

TREAT YOURSELF Get a milkshake at Pleasant Valley Shake Shoppe on Pleasant Valley Road, about 6 miles from the trailhead.

The Earl H. Barnhart "Buzzard's Roost" Nature Preserve
(740) 773-8794
Facebook @rosscoparkdistrict

Stay straight past the yellow Chilo Trail before reaching an open meadow with prairie flowers and a pond. There are restrooms here and a covered bench, which is nice for quiet reflection. Continue straight on South Point Trail toward the ridgeline, passing Blueberry Trail on your left. Use caution; the cliff edges are steep and dangerous. The views are remarkable, overlooking hundreds of acres of hills, woodlands, and the creek. In winter, you may spot deer or foxes in the valley. Look in the sky and trees for the vultures that give this park its name. Cross a creek and waterfall, then reach the main Paint Creek lookout. A flat rock juts out, providing unobstructed views of the valley. Pass Blueberry Trail on your left, cross a creek, and pass a great overlook. Stay straight past the yellow Chilo Trail and return to the trailhead. Consider camping nearby at the Shawnee Valley Campground.

SCAVENGER HUNT

Leaves falling up

"In fall, when the sun is rising and heating up the south-facing cliffs, the falling leaves actually fall upward due to air currents rising up the cliff walls!" says Ranger Joe Letsche. Can you spot leaves rising rather than falling?

Trail on the ridgeline

Black cherry

This is the largest of the wild cherry trees and easy to identify by its dark grayish-black crackled bark. Many species of birds like its black berries, and people use them to make jams, jellies, and liqueurs. The bark is even used in some cough syrups. Have you ever tried cherry-flavored jams or medicine?

Prunus serotina

Vulture

Buzzards Roost is named for the two species of vultures seen here: turkey and black vultures. Turkey vultures have long "fingers" at their wing-tips. They hold their wings slightly raised, making a V and flying in circles. Black vultures are smaller, with a bare black head and more power-ful wingbeats. Turkey vultures have a better sense of smell, so black vultures often hang around them to find food, which is mostly dead animals. Spread your arms into a V and "fly" like a vulture.

Turkey vulture (*Cathartes aura*) in flight and black vultures (*Coragyps atratus*)

Red fox

These mammals like open woodlands, brushy fields, and even suburban neighborhoods. They're very adaptable, often thought to be clever and sneaky for their ability to steal food from farms. Their excellent hearing helps them hunt. They can even hear rodents digging underground.

Vulpes vulpes

Broom forkmoss

Unlike most other plants, mosses don't have roots. Instead, they have hairlike structures that anchor to rocks, bark, or soil. There are up to 25,000 different species of moss, and they live on every continent on the planet! They help soak up rain and keep moisture in the soil. Give it a gentle touch. What does it feel like?

Dicranum scoparium

44

CHASE WATERFALLS AT ENGLEWOOD METROPARK

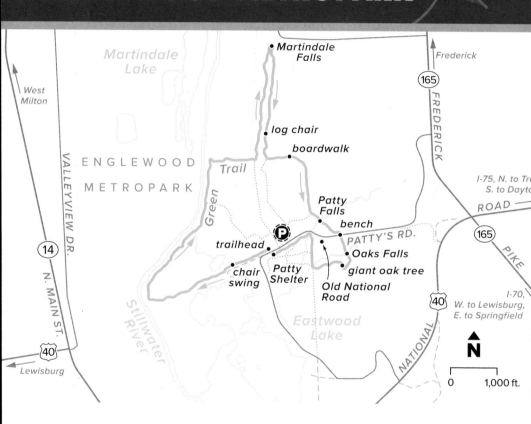

YOUR ADVENTURE

Adventurers, today you'll explore forests on the historical homeland of the Miami. Head left from the Patty Shelter and Eastwood Lake, following the green trail blazes. Power up at the chair swing overlooking Eastwood Lake, then cross a bridge. The trail along the Stillwater River is lined with wildflowers and trees like hackberry and sycamore. It can be muddy, making it

This trail features three waterfalls →

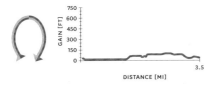

GAIN [FT]

750
600
450
300
150
0

DISTANCE [MI]

3.5

LENGTH 3.5-mile loop

ELEVATION GAIN 210 feet

HIKE TIME + EXPLORE 2.5–3 hours

DIFFICULTY Moderate—longer, with a couple of inclines

SEASON Year-round. Spring is good for wildflowers, winter for frozen waterfalls when the weather is right.

GET THERE Take OH-48 / Main Street north through Dayton to turn right onto US-40. Turn left into the Englewood Park entrance and follow Patty's Road and park near the Patty Shelter and picnic area with a playground. The trailhead begins near Eastwood Lake.

Google Maps: bit.ly/englewoodgreentrail

RESTROOM At trailhead

FEE None

TREAT YOURSELF Stop for cupcakes and coffee at Stone House Sweets Bakery & Coffee House, located 2.5 miles away on Union Boulevard.

Englewood MetroPark
(937) 275-7275
Facebook @FiveRiversMetroparks

a great place to look for animal tracks. Pass the White Trail on your right. The trail turns away from the river and takes a sharp left. Enter thicker woods and cross a creek, soon arriving at Martindale Falls. Spend some time here, then climb the stairs and turn right. Pass a log seat and reach a junction with the Yellow Trail—turn left onto the Green Trail. Reach a boardwalk through a pumpkin ash and swamp forest. This site is protected as a national landmark because the trees are so rare. Reach a bench and overlook of Patty Falls. The trail winds down and crosses the top—stay straight on Green, past the Purple Trail. Stairs lead down to a view of the falls. Cross Old National Road to a bridge, where you'll spot Oaks Falls. Near the massive oak tree, reach a junction. Turn right, following the path lined by walnut, maple, oak, linden, and locust trees. Pass a couple of Blue Trail connectors and benches. Continue straight to an old stone bridge over Old National Road again. Turn left, paralleling the road. Reach the play area and Patty Shelter, where you began. Stay for the weekend at the nearby Patty Hollow Campsite.

SCAVENGER HUNT

Historical bridge

This stone bridge was part of the original National Road, the first major US highway built by the federal government. It was constructed in 1811 and ran between Maryland and Illinois. In the mid-1800s, it was an important transportation corridor moving people, goods, and livestock. Imagine living before cars were invented. How long would it take to cross several states by horse and carriage?

Remnants from the first highway

Pumpkin ash

Four species of these deciduous (loses its leaves) trees are common in Ohio, but this species is extremely rare. It's critically endangered (meaning it's almost extinct), so this remnant swamp forest of rare trees is special. Arborists (tree specialists) are working to protect them from an invasive bug called the emerald ash borer that is threatening them. This tree gets its name from its swollen, pumpkin-shaped base. Draw this rare tree in your nature journal.

Fraxinus profunda

Deer tracks

Look down and you might spot an animal track, like this deer print. Animals like deer, raccoons, foxes, coyotes, opossums, and skunks live here. Muddy areas near the river are a great place to look for tracks. Deer hooves appear as two symmetrical halves, like a heart. Be an animal tracker—which way do you think it went?

Odocoileus virginianus tracks

Northern cardinal

This is Ohio's state bird. The males are bright red and named after the religious figures who wear red robes. Cardinals are like flamingos; they get their color pigment from the foods they eat. What foods do you think contribute to their color? What color would you be if your body were influenced by what you ate?

Cardinalis cardinalis

45

EXPERIENCE NATURE'S HEALING IN GLEN HELEN NATURE PRESERVE

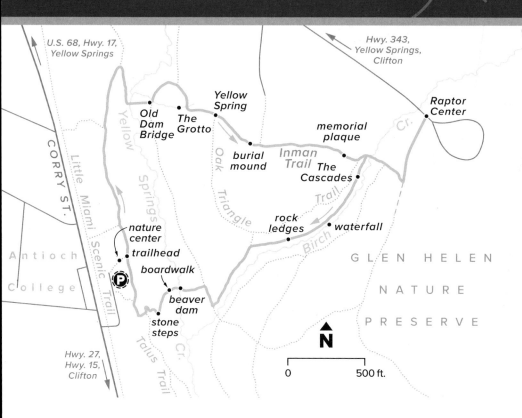

YOUR ADVENTURE

Adventurers, today you'll go on a beautiful nature trek that is filled with myth and lore, on the historical homeland of the Miami. Begin by going left at the trailhead behind the Trailside Museum and Vernet Ecological Center. Curve right (staying straight past left offshoots) and reach a bridge to The Grotto, a small cave behind a waterfall. Turn left here on Inman

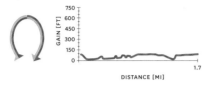

LENGTH 1.7-mile loop

ELEVATION GAIN 131 feet

HIKE TIME + EXPLORE 1–1.5 hours

DIFFICULTY Easy—well-maintained path with just a bit of elevation; can add segments for energetic or older kids

SEASON Year-round, but especially lovely in April and May when wildflowers bloom.

GET THERE From US-68 in Yellow Springs, take Limestone Street east for 0.8 miles. Turn right onto Corry Street, and Glen Helen Nature Preserve is immediately on the left. Park in the lot.

Google Maps: bit.ly/timberglenhelen

RESTROOM At trailhead

FEE $5 day parking/free for Glen Helen Members

TREAT YOURSELF Farm fresh treats and fun await you at Young's Jersey Dairy, 2.5 miles from the preserve.

Glen Helen Nature Preserve
(937) 769-1902
Facebook @GlenHelen

Trail as it curves right, and reach the unusual, colorful spring that the town of Yellow Springs was named for. This water is legendary for its supposed healing powers. Today, people still visit the spring for healing, but some of its mysteries have been solved by science. Due to contaminants leaching into it from nearby industry and farms, the water is not considered safe to drink. Continue straight and see an ancient burial mound from the Hopewell people who lived here long before the Miami. Notice the size of the trees around you; some ancient oaks here date back four hundred years. Soon come to a bridge over The Cascades waterfall. Cross it, then turn left, following the trail to the Raptor Center, which houses rescued eagles, hawks, and owls. Head back the way you came, crossing back over the bridge. Turn left on Inman Trail and follow it to The Cascades lookout under a rock ledge. Go left down stairs to a creek. Turn right and reach a bridge and boardwalk over Yellow Springs Creek. Look right for the large beaver dam, then climb the stairs back to the trailhead. Make it a weekend and camp at the nearby John Bryan State Park Campground.

SCAVENGER HUNT

Yellow Springs

Why do you think the water at this spring stains everything around it an orange-yellow color? The answer is rust! An aquifer with high levels of iron feeds this spring. When the iron in the water mixes with oxygen in the air, it produces rust.

Healing waters

Seasonal special: liverwort

Look for the white, blue, or pink flowers of *Hepatica* in early spring. Its stems are furry— run your hands along them.

Hepatica nobilis

Burial mound

Two thousand years ago, people of an advanced culture, known as the Hopewell, lived here. They made large, complex ceremonial and burial mounds. Only a few remain today in protected areas like this one. Quietly reflect here and think about someone you care about.

Hopewell mound

Ancient oaks

If these deciduous (lose their leaves) trees could talk, imagine the stories they could tell! The thicker and taller they are, the older they are. Some were here before European pilgrims arrived in the New World. Use your imagination. If these trees could tell you a story, what do you think they would share?

Quercus alba

Raptor rescue

Many raptors live here, including owls, hawks, eagles, and falcons. Sometimes they get sick or injured and need help. The Glen Helen Raptor Center is the only medical care facility in the region that can nurse them to health. Look overhead for wild raptors, or visit the Raptor Center to see some up close.

Barred owl (*Strix varia*) and bald eagle (*Haliaeetus leucocephalus*)

46

CROSS THE SWINGING BRIDGE IN CAESAR CREEK STATE PARK

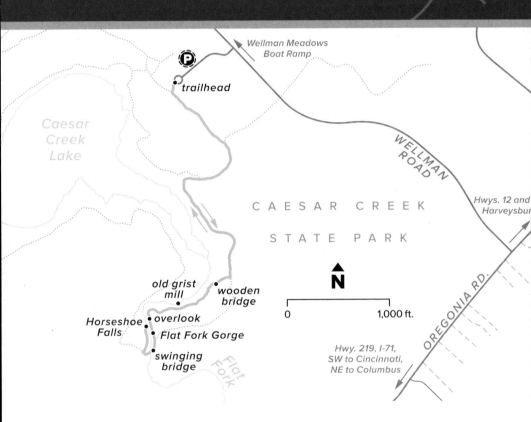

Wellman Meadows
Boat Ramp

trailhead

Caesar
Creek
Lake

WELLMAN ROAD

Hwys. 12 and
Harveysbur

CAESAR CREEK

STATE PARK

N

old grist
mill

wooden
bridge

Horseshoe
Falls

overlook

Flat Fork Gorge

0   1,000 ft.

swinging
bridge

Flat Fork

Hwy. 219, I-71,
SW to Cincinnati,
NE to Columbus

OREGONIA RD.

YOUR ADVENTURE

Adventurers, today you're exploring a forest and waterway on the historical homeland of the Miami. Begin at the Wellman trailhead. When the trail splits, go left, following the blue blazes. Along the trail, signs will highlight a variety of tree species—try to spot them, matching the leaves to the drawings provided. Stay straight at a trail junction and cross a bridge. At the next

Enjoy these falls year round →

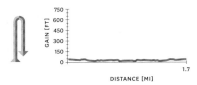

GAIN [FT]

DISTANCE [MI]

LENGTH 1.7-mile out and back

ELEVATION GAIN 75 feet

HIKE TIME + EXPLORE 1.5 hours

DIFFICULTY Easy—mostly flat trail

SEASON Year-round. Summer is fun for splashing in the falls.

GET THERE From Lebanon, take Oregonia Road to the Caesar Creek State Park

entrance. Turn left after half a mile and park in the lot at the Wellman trailhead.

Google Maps: bit.ly/timberhorseshoefalls

RESTROOM At trailhead (closed in winter)

FEE None

TREAT YOURSELF Grab a bite at Butter Churn Cafe & Young's Hand Dipped Ice Cream, located on Main Street about 4 miles from the park.

Caesar Creek State Park
(513) 897-3055
Facebook @Caesarcreekstatepark

fork, turn right. Stay right to follow the blue blazes, cross a bridge, and take stairs down to the creek and an overlook. Look carefully to see the remnants from an old grist mill. Next, reach the impressive Flat Fork Gorge with its enormous stone ledge. There are picnic tables here. It's a nice place to power up and explore the shallow creek bed. Just past the gorge, reach the first viewpoint for Horseshoe Falls. At another intersection, stay straight and reach the swinging bridge that spans Flat Fork Creek. Cross the bridge, then turn right, following the sign to Horseshoe Falls. Spend some time enjoying the falls, then head back the same way you came. There is more to explore in this park, including a pioneer village, nature center, and lake. Consider camping at Caesar Creek State Park Campground.

SCAVENGER HUNT

Eastern cottonwood

These shady trees produce a signature fluffy white cotton-like seed that floats through the air from late April through June. You can also identify this tree by its heart-shaped leaves with serrated edges. Collect as many as you can from the ground and make a mosaic pattern out of them.

Populus deltoides (means "triangle" in Latin, for its leaves)

Red-tailed hawk

These birds of prey have great vision. They like to eat mice and other small mammals, and can spot them from 100 feet in the air. Do an experiment with your trail mate. Stand still while your trail mate walks one hundred steps away down the trail. That is how far away a hawk can see a mouse! If you don't see a hawk while on the trail, stop by the nature center, where they have one in their care.

Buteo jamaicensis

Osage orange

These large round green fruits drop to the ground in fall. They have many names based on what people think they look like. They aren't related to oranges, despite their most common name, nor are they apples, though some call them hedge apples. Pick one up from the ground. What does it look and feel like to you?

Maclura pomifera

Mink

These mammals live near streams and ponds. Their fur is coated in oil to repel water. Your best chance for seeing mink is in the early morning or early evening. They are crepuscular, which means active at dusk and dawn. Do you feel more active in the morning or evening?

Neogale vison

Swinging bridge

Steady your legs and hold onto the ropes as you cross this fun swinging bridge over a stream that flows into Caesar Creek. Try to resist the urge to shake your hike mates off it as you cross. It's also known as a "simple suspension bridge"—it has only cables anchored at either end of the stream. Think about how many bridges you've seen on your adventures so far—which has been your favorite?

The bridge spans 100 feet and was completed in 2015

47

WET YOUR FEET AT INDIAN CREEK METROPARK

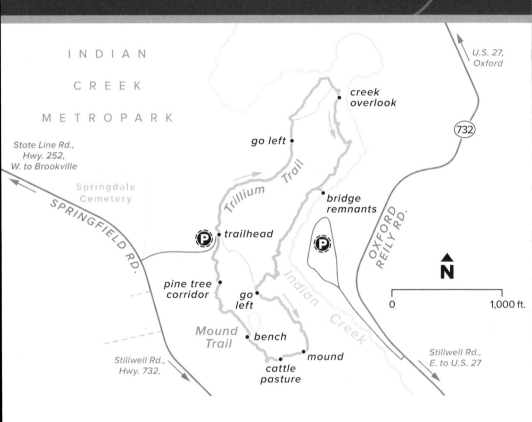

INDIAN

CREEK

METROPARK

State Line Rd.,
Hwy. 252,
W. to Brookville

Springdale
Cemetery

SPRINGFIELD RD.

Trillium Trail

creek overlook

go left

bridge remnants

trailhead

pine tree corridor

go left

Mound Trail

bench

mound

cattle pasture

Stillwell Rd.,
Hwy. 732,

Indian Creek

U.S. 27,
Oxford

732

OXFORD REILY RD.

Stillwell Rd.,
E. to U.S. 27

N

0   1,000 ft.

YOUR ADVENTURE

Adventurers, today you'll explore a trail on the historical homeland of the Miami. Begin by walking along a grassy walkway that was once a road. Reach Trillium Trailhead and enter the shady forest of maple, oak, and hickory trees as you make your way toward Indian Creek. You'll see the creek, and then the trail will curve right. Reach a great overlook of the

Explore forests and the creek along Trillium Trail →

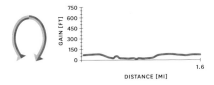

GAIN [FT]

750
600
450
300
150
0

1.6

DISTANCE [MI]

LENGTH 1.6-mile loop

ELEVATION GAIN 121 feet

HIKE TIME + EXPLORE 1.5 hours

DIFFICULTY Moderate—a little incline, and stairs

SEASON Year-round. Spring is ideal for woodland wildflowers, and summer for getting your feet wet and fossil hunting in Indian Creek.

GET THERE From Oxford, take OH-732 S / Oxford Reily Road to where it becomes Main Street, then continue onto Springfield Road. Indian Creek MetroPark entrance is on the right. Park in the lot. Signage for the Trillium Trail is left of the playground.

Google Maps: bit.ly/timbertrilliumtrail

RESTROOM At trailhead

FEE Free for Butler County residents; motor vehicle permits are $15 for nonresidents and can be purchased at YourMetroParks.net

TREAT YOURSELF Grab some soft-serve ice cream with an exhaustive list of flavors and toppings at Spring Street Treats in Oxford, about 6.5 miles from the trail.

Indian Creek MetroPark
(513) 867-5835
Facebook @metroparks

creek below. This one is quite steep—use extra caution near the edge. Follow the creek, spotting species that thrive along waterways, like riverbank grape, sycamore, and many wildflowers in spring, including the one the trail is named for—trillium. Descend to creek level on a small offshoot to the water's edge. Power up, explore the shallow water, and hunt for fossils. Follow the trail across a small stream to some stairs. Climb back up and go right, then curve left, following the blazes. Reach an open area with a distinctive mound—a re-creation of an ancient burial or ceremonial mound that native peoples built in this area. Now pass a pasture—you might even spot a cow! Reach a bench overlooking a spring-fed pond. Take a minute to rest and observe, watching for birds and amphibians in this area. Then the trail leads through a beautiful, towering white pine forest, creating a cathedral of trees. When you exit the corridor, the trail ends at the parking area.

SCAVENGER HUNT

Yellow warbler

These are the most brilliantly colored and easy to spot native warblers in the area. Abundant in spring and summer, they leave Ohio by August to head south for winter. Their song sounds like *sweet, sweet, sweet, sweeter than sweet!* Can you sing like a songbird?

Setophaga petechia

Oyster mushroom

Oyster mushrooms are unique shell-shaped fungi that grow year-round. Unlike most fungi that eat decaying plant material, this mushroom is a carnivore! It poisons, paralyzes, and consumes roundworms. Do you know the difference between a carnivore and herbivore?

Pleurotus ostreatus

Acorn plum gall wasp

These plum-colored balls look like fruit, but they're actually home to a wasp larva living inside. The balls are an abnormal growth, called a gall, formed by the tree after a wasp lays her egg. The gall grows around the larva to protect it; it's harmless to the tree. What do you do at home to stay safe?

Amphibolips quercusjuglans

Pawpaw

These deciduous (lose their leaves) trees are prevalent throughout Ohio. They love moist creek banks. Look for their large, simple, oblong leaves. This tropical-type plant produces the largest edible fruit native to North America. They look like small green potatoes. Can you name another fruit that grows locally?

Asimina triloba ("triple-lobed" in Latin)

Riverbank grape

There are several species of wild grapes in Ohio. The most common is riverbank grape. Look for the twisty vines that grow on and around trees and can climb over fifty feet. They have white blooms in early summer and dark blue to purple fruits by early fall. Wildlife love this fruit, but don't ever eat anything you find in nature without an adult because some poisonous plants look similar. How many colors and flavors of grapes can you name?

Vitis riparia fruit

48

TAKE THE GORGE-OUS FITNESS CHALLENGE AT SHARON WOODS

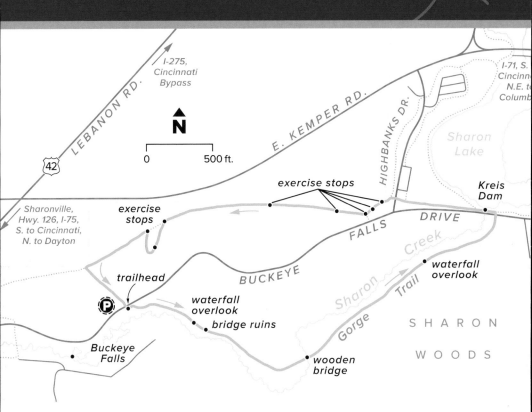

YOUR ADVENTURE

Adventurers, today you'll spot multiple waterfalls on the historical home-land of the Miami. This is a state nature preserve because of its native plant and animal communities and its geology. Begin on the Gorge Trail. QR codes along the path provide audio interpretation to enrich your learning. Reach the first waterfall overlook. Notice the layers of bedrock exposed,

There are multiple waterfalls along this trail →

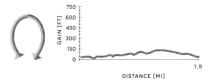

GAIN [FT]

DISTANCE [MI]

LENGTH 1.9-mile loop

ELEVATION GAIN 171

HIKE TIME + EXPLORE 1–1.5 hours

DIFFICULTY Easy—minimal elevation

SEASON Year-round. Spring has wild-flowers; summer has jewelweed and asters; fall has foliage and cooler temps.

GET THERE From Cincinnati, take US-42 / Lebanon Drive north to Sharon Woods Drive. Turn left on Buckeye Falls Drive and follow it for 0.4 miles. Park in the lot on the left. The trailhead for the Gorge Trail is right across the road.

Google Maps: bit.ly/timbergorgetrail

RESTROOM On Buckeye Falls Drive, about 0.25 miles before trailhead

FEE $5/car for Hamilton County residents; $8/car for nonresidents; annual passes available at GreatParks.org/shop

TREAT YOURSELF Try a frozen treat at Rhino's Frozen Yogurt and Soft Serve, about 4 miles away on Kenwood Road.

Sharon Woods Park
(513) 521-7275
Facebook @GreatParksHC

as well as boulders carried here from as far away as Canada by the glacier. Next, spot the ruins of an old footbridge that once spanned Sharon Creek. Watch for birds, as this is a great birding trail. Next, cross the creek on a bridge, before reaching an overlook. Come to another impressive water- fall with another overlook. Now make your way toward the historical Kreis Dam. The Gorge Trail ends at Sharon Lake. Turn left and walk over the dam and down the stairs to view the arched stone architecture. Then head back up and cross Buckeye Falls Drive toward the lake. Turn left and follow the trail uphill. Cross Highbanks Drive and turn left to the Fitness Trail, lined by maple and walnut trees. It features different fitness activ- ities at each stop, like touching your toes or jumping jacks. Take a short horseshoe-shaped trail with another fitness station, and reconnect to the main path. Follow the trail to the picnic area near where you began, turning left at the connection path back to the parking lot. For more fun, visit the heritage village near the trailhead (for a fee). Find more information at HeritageVillageCincinnati.org.

SCAVENGER HUNT

Kreis Dam

During the Great Depression, the Kreis Dam was built to provide greater recreational opportunities for the public. Rocks from the creek bed were

used where the lake would be, and they dammed Sharon Creek to create a 30-acre lake. Beavers are also great dam builders. Try an experiment at home. Build a dam using sand, rocks, and popsicle sticks in a plastic tub. Construct your dam, then pour water in to see if it holds.

The dam was built in 1936

Belted kingfisher

This bird has a large head and a long bill and frequently makes a rattling call when it flies. Look for them perched on trees near water. They eat fish, amphibians, insects, and small reptiles and crustaceans. A group of belted kingfishers isn't called a flock, it's called a rattle. Can you name three other types of animal groupings?

Megaceryle alcyon

Black maple

Fall foliage is fabulous on this trail, thanks to the maple trees. Black maple is a subspecies of sugar maple, with slightly darker bark and three-lobed leaves, instead of five-lobed. It hosts around three hundred insect species, mostly caterpillars, so birds love this tree. Sugar maples are famous for a sweet treat humans like—do you know what it is?

Acer nigrum

Wood duck

These are one of the few American ducks that can perch and nest in trees. They sometimes nest in abandoned woodpecker holes or use nesting boxes

put up by rangers. The males, called drakes, are the most colorful ducks in North America. They have red eyes and many shimmering colors on their head. How many colors do you see on this bird?

Aix sponsa

49

SEE EPIC VIEWS AT BENDER MOUNTAIN

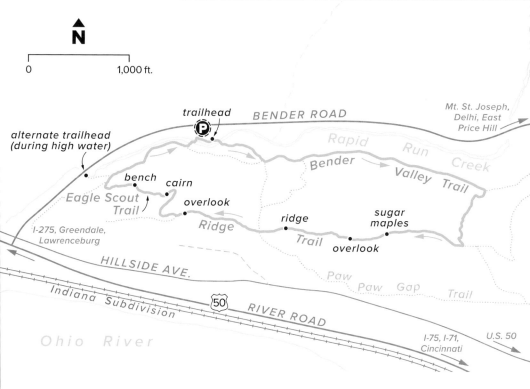

N

0   1,000 ft.

trailhead

BENDER ROAD

Mt. St. Joseph, Delhi, East Price Hill

alternate trailhead (during high water)

Rapid

Run

Creek

Bender

Valley

Trail

bench   cairn

Eagle Scout Trail

overlook

ridge

sugar maples

I-275, Greendale, Lawrenceburg

Ridge

Trail

overlook

HILLSIDE AVE.

Paw   Paw   Gap   Trail

Indiana Subdivision

50

RIVER ROAD

I-75, I-71, Cincinnati

U.S. 50

Ohio River

YOUR ADVENTURE

Adventurers, today you'll climb to one of the highest ridgelines in the region for a view of the Ohio River, on the historical homeland of the Miami. Cross Rapid Run Creek and go straight to the wayfinder sign, then go left on Bender Valley Trail and follow the pink blazes. Wind through a field of waterleaf, wild ginger, monkey grass, and pawpaws. At a connection to the

Epic ridgeline hike with views →

LENGTH 2.4-mile loop

ELEVATION GAIN 390 feet

HIKE TIME + EXPLORE 2 hours

DIFFICULTY Challenging—longer, with elevation gain and steep, rugged terrain

SEASON Year-round.

GET THERE Take US-50 / Ohio River Scenic Byway / River Road west through Cincinnati to turn right on Bender Road and drive 0.4 miles to the small parking area and trailhead on the right.

Google Maps: bit.ly/timberbendermountain

RESTROOM At gas station about 1.5 miles northwest of trailhead on US-50

FEE None

TREAT YOURSELF Enjoy a famous Cincinnati dessert at Graeter's Ice Cream, about 5 miles away on Westbourne Drive.

Bender Mountain Nature Preserve
(513) 921-9453
Facebook @WesternWildlifeCorridor

Paw Paw Gap Trail, stay straight on Bender Valley Trail as it turns into Ridge Trail. At a wayfinder sign, turn right toward the ridge overlooking the Ohio River, where you can see out to Kentucky. Turn right through a forest of maple trees that are brilliant yellow in fall. Watch for the root ball of a massive tree that is being decomposed by mushrooms. As you progress, the trail gets extremely narrow and steep on both sides. The ridgeline puts you eye-to-eye with the treetops, providing a rare view of life in the canopy of massive oak, maple, and hickory trees. Pass an overlook and a bench at the intersection of the Paw Paw Gap Trail. Stay straight here. Pay special attention to the bird life rarely glimpsed from this vantage point. Cut right and descend down the hillside, then turn right on Eagle Scout Trail just after a bench. Pass a large rock cairn with children's trinkets, and a bench. Near the bottom, at the connection for the Bender Valley Trail, turn right. Continue straight to the first junction you arrived at with North Paw Paw Gap—turn left and cross the creek back to the trailhead.

SCAVENGER HUNT

Sweetgum

The scientific name for this tree literally translates to "liquid amber" because of its fragrant gum or juice, which has been used historically to

make chewing gum. Recognize it by its five-pointed, star-shaped leaves. Also look for the spiky round gumballs that drop in fall. Finches and chipmunks love this fruit. Gently touch one of the balls. How do you think animals get the seeds out with all those spikes?

Liquidambar styraciflua

Bluntleaf waterleaf

This rare low-growing woodland plant is threatened or endangered in several states. You can find it growing along the trail on Bender Mountain. The dark green leaves are shaped like a maple leaf. In late spring, you'll notice white to lavender blossoms in clusters. Draw this rare find in your nature journal.

Hydrophyllum canadense

Blue jay

Look in the trees for blue, and listen closely for the loud "jay" calls of this very vocal bird. One of their favorite foods is acorns, so oak trees are a good place to look. Jays warn other birds about nearby predators by imitating the sound of a hawk when they spot one. Can you imitate one of your hike mates?

Cyanocitta cristata

Eastern garter snake

You may spot this harmless reptile along the trail. How they got their common name is unclear. They were possibly named because their colorful

stripe resembles garters, which were used to hold up socks. Or their name comes from the German word for "garden" because people often find them in their gardens. Snakes smell with their tongue. Stick out your tongue and flick it like a snake. Do you smell anything?

Thamnophis sirtalis

EXPLORE MYSTERIES AT SERPENT MOUND

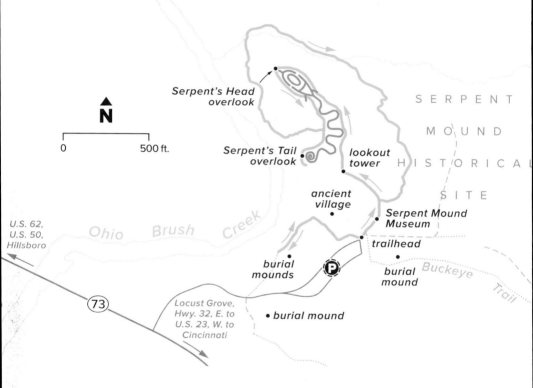

N

0   500 ft.

Serpent's Head overlook

Serpent's Tail overlook

lookout tower

ancient village

Serpent Mound Museum

trailhead

burial mounds

burial mound

U.S. 62, U.S. 50, Hillsboro

Ohio   Brush   Creek

73

Locust Grove, Hwy. 32, E. to U.S. 23, W. to Cincinnati

• burial mound

Buckeye Trail

S E R P E N T   M O U N D   H I S T O R I C A L   S I T E

YOUR ADVENTURE

Adventurers, today you're on the historical homeland of the Adena and Fort Ancient cultures. You'll see the world's largest surviving example of an ancient animal effigy mound, built by ancient Native Americans thousands of years ago. The Serpent Mound stretches 1400 feet and is beautifully preserved. This area is also geologically significant. Three hundred million

Explore ancient history and culture →

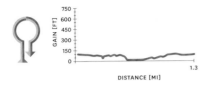

GAIN [FT]

750
600
450
300
150
0

1.3

DISTANCE [MI]

LENGTH 1.3-mile lollipop loop

ELEVATION GAIN 121 feet

HIKE TIME + EXPLORE 1–1.5 hours

DIFFICULTY Moderate—rugged and somewhat steep dirt trail; flat and easy paved path around Serpent Mound

SEASON Mid-March to mid-November; the summer solstice offers a unique experience at this site.

GET THERE From SR 41 N / N Main Street in Peebles, turn left on OH-73 W and follow it for 3.9 miles. The entrance to Serpent Mound is on the right. The trail begins behind the museum.

Google Maps: bit.ly/timberserpentmound

RESTROOM At trailhead

FEE $8 per car

TREAT YOURSELF Grab lunch at Tomahawk Pizza, located about 4 miles away on OH-41.

Serpent Mound Historical Site
(937) 587-2796
Facebook @SerpentMound

years ago, a meteorite blew apart miles of rock, creating a four-mile-wide circular crater. You'll explore a portion of it along the Brush Creek Nature Trail. Begin at the museum, then head to the mound. Signs explain the theories, culture, and history of this sacred place. Go right past the lookout tower toward the serpent's head. It's perfectly aligned to the setting sun of the summer solstice; many historians believe this is intentional. Continue toward the serpent's tail, where there is a bench and observation point. Power up here, and look down to the creek, where you're heading next. Head left back toward the trailhead, then turn left on Brush Creek Trail toward Ohio Brush Creek. The trail can be muddy at times and a little steep. You'll see unique rock formations caused by the ancient asteroid. Cross two bridges, taking time to enjoy the water and look for birds and aquatic species. Follow the trail back up the ridge, where it ends behind the museum. Turn left back toward the parking lot. Spot a burial mound to your left, then walk to the right of the parking lot to the site of an ancient village and multiple burial mounds with information about their creation.

SCAVENGER HUNT

Wild turkeys

Wild turkeys were prolific in Ohio prior to European settlement. Prehistoric Native Americans domesticated them nearly 3000 years ago to use their

feathers for robes and blankets, and their bones for tools. Turkeys could no longer be found here by 1904 due to unregulated hunting and loss of habitat, but thanks to recovery efforts, they are back. The hens (females) yelp to communicate. Other sounds include clucks, purrs, putts, cackles, and even a *kee-kee* if they get lost. How many sounds can you make?

Meleagris gallopavo

Burial mounds

Near Serpent Mound are multiple burial mounds from the Adena and Fort Ancient cultures, dating back hundreds or thousands of years. Respectfully walk the grounds of this sacred site. How many burial mounds can you find? Try to imagine what life was like here that long ago.

Adena mound

Ghost trees

American sycamores are sometimes called ghost trees because of their white branches near the crown. This is especially evident in fall when their leaves turn bright orange against the white bark. They're the largest leaves of any tree in North America! Find a fallen leaf and hold it up to your head. Which is bigger?

Leaf and bark of *Platanus occidentalis*

Queensnake

Ohio has twenty species of snakes, most harmless to people. The ancient mound builders honored them. The queensnake is aquatic and likes shallow, slow-moving water. Look along the trail and around the creek and maybe you'll spot a snake—but never touch. If you find one, draw it in your nature journal.

Regina septemvittata

ACKNOWLEDGMENTS

There is nothing more reaffirming that we live in a world full of caring people than when hard-working rangers, parents, conservationists, biologists, geologists, and hikers call us back or respond to our emails, helping us get that species identification just right or helping us verify the year a major discovery happened on the trail. Special thanks to Jacqueline Gerling and Ralph Protano, Cleveland Metroparks; Joe Letsche, Ross County Park District; Heidi Hetzel-Evans, Ohio Department of Natural Resources; Bridgett Hernandez and Evan Hill, ACRES Land Trust; Marion Mason, Hoosier National Forest; Andrea Crain and Suzanne Hirsch, Shawnee National Forest; Greg O'Neil, Mill Creek Park; Maritza Rocha and Stacina Stagner, Cook County Forest Preserve District; Laurie Freeman, Betty Ross, Nick Boutis, Rebecca Jaramillo, and Jesse Post, Glen Helen Nature Preserve; Deb Humiston, Jay Johnson, and Glenn Perricone, Dupage County Forest Preserve District; Ginger Murphy, Marty Benson, and Tom Swinford, Indiana Natural Resources Department; Teresa Rody, Mississinewa State Park; Dylan Allison, Fort Harrison State Park; Jeremy Beavin, Charlestown State Park; Sheree Belt, Spring Mill State Park; Doug Baird, Brown County State Park; Kayla Leach Wilson, Clifty Falls State Park; Aaron Douglass, Shades and Turkey Run State Parks; Don Nicholls, Hamilton County Parks and Recreation; Eden Lamb and Maria Sutherland, Lindenwood Nature Preserve; Morgan Kelley, Mounds State Park; Mary Rozum and Tim Sisson, Western Wildlife Corridor/Bender Mountain Nature Preserve; Nikki Ferrell, Great Parks of Hamilton County; Molie Oliver, Cache River State Natural Area; Chris Ashley, Kelleys Island State Park; Richelle Gatto, Nelson Kennedy Ledges State Park; Jenna Winters and Lauren (Broddrick) Stewart, Maumee Bay State Park; Amy Pellman, MetroParks of Butler County; Kody Kirby, McCormick's Creek State Park; Jennifer Randolph Bollinger, Giant City State Park; Lisa Sons, Starved Rock and Matthiessen State Parks; Chris Hespen, Pere Marquette State Park; Jacob Shurpit, Moraine Hills State Park; Jayette Bolins, Illinois Department of Natural Resources; Savannah Robles, Dave Dyer, and Brad Lepper, Ohio

History Connection; Dave Pittman, Friends of Rocky Glen; Lauren Lemons, Five River MetroParks; Jill Weiss Simins, Indiana Historical Bureau; Chris Benda, Southern Illinois University; Alison Price, Lincoln Park Zoo; Rebecca Jones Macko, Cuyahoga Valley National Park; Todd Thompson, Indiana Geological & Water Survey; and Sara Lesire and Laura Tolbert.

Huge thanks to Stacee Lawrence, Cobi Lawson, Mike Dempsey, Andrew Beckman, Hillary Caudle, Sarah Crumb, Sarah Milhollin, David Deis, Melina Hughes, Kathryn Juergens, and the entire Timber Press family for believing in a new volume to help reach Midwestern families!

To Wendy's family—to Gail, Xavier, and Jaedon Moore for being my trusty guinea pigs; to my father, Alan, for being an amazing driver and hiker; to my husband, Garrison, for being head GPS tracker, cheerleader, and chef; and to my mother, Ginny, for her research skills. This book is about family, and having a strong family supporting you makes adventure possible.

To Sharon's family—to my kids, Kaelan and Siena, for always reminding me to never underestimate what kids can accomplish, and for always being enthusiastic—even when we go on three hikes a day. You marvel at nature and reinforce why this book is so beneficial. To my husband, Alex, for being our Eagle Scout, always prepared and always supportive every step of the way. And to my mom, Barb, and late father, Robert, for taking me tent camping as a kid, reinforcing a love of the great outdoors and a passion for writing.

And thanks to all of you for reading this and getting outside with each other! We can't wait to see the adventures you go on.

PHOTO AND ILLUSTRATION CREDITS

All photos are by the authors with the exception of those listed below.
Maps by David Deis
Illustrations by Always With Honor

Map on page 48 Courtesy of David
Rumsey Map Collection, David
Rumsey Map Center, Stanford
Libraries. *Map of the States Of
Ohio Indiana & Illinois And Part
Of Michigan Territory Compiled
from the Latest Authorities*. Drawn
by D.H. Vance end engraved
by J.H. Young. Philadelphia:
Published by Anthony Finley 1826.

Anna / Adobe Stock, 141
Annado / Shutterstock, 142 top
arthurgphotography /
Shutterstock, 137
Chris Ashley, 209 middle and bottom
Courtesy of Kelleys Island
State Park, 208 bottom
Courtesy of the Mounds Sate
Park Archives, 183 bottom
Ej Rodriquez Photography
/ Dreamstime, 91

Jesse Post / Glen Helen Nature
Reserve, 245 bottom left,
245 bottom right
Kazakovmaksim / iStock, 54
Matt Weldon, 191 bottom
Michael John Maniurski /
Shutterstock, 92 bottom
publicdomainpictures.net/jks Lola, 53
Thomas Sprunger, Acres
Land Trust, 191 top
Todd Bannor / Alamy, 167 middle

WikiMedia
Public Domain
Andrew King/USFWS Midwest
Region, 163 top
Jacob W. Frank/NPS, 88
Joanne Redwood, 237 middle right
Keenan Adams/USFWS, 229 middle
Lynn Betts / Photo courtesy of USDA
Natural Resources Conservation
Service, 135 middle, 264 bottom

INDEX

ABOUT YOUR LEAD ADVENTURERS

© Jamilla Yip

SHARON was raised in Ohio and is raising her kids in Illinois. She is a US Navy veteran, holds a master's degree in communications management and an undergraduate degree in psychology, and has worked in public relations and journalism for more than two decades. Her passion for wildlife and nature conservation led her to a career working with zoological professionals at San Diego Zoo Wildlife Alliance and Lincoln Park Zoo in Chicago. Today, she is an award-winning communications consultant at Public Communications Inc., an independent agency in Chicago specializing in communications for environmental leaders, wildlife scientists, and animal health professionals nationwide. She also serves on the board of directors for the national chimpanzee sanctuary, Chimp Haven. Sharon believes strongly in the healing power of nature and the important role that travel and exploration play in shaping our lives. Not only do she and her family enjoy getting outdoors often, but they also love traveling, both regionally and globally. She strives to make nature outings and family travel more welcoming and accessible by sharing tips and experiences, encouraging parents to explore with their children. Follow her family's adventures on Instagram @shazfamilytravels and email shazfamilytravels@gmail.com.

© Boone Rodriguez

WENDY holds a master's degree in learning technologies and is a former classroom teacher. As part of her quest to bring science education alive, she worked as a National Geographic Fellow in Australia researching Tasmanian devils, a PolarTREC teacher researcher in archaeology in Alaska, an Earthwatch teacher fellow in the Bahamas and New Orleans, and a GoNorth! teacher explorer studying climate change via dogsled in Finland, Norway, and Sweden. Today, she is a global education consultant who has traveled to more than fifty countries to design programs, build communities, and inspire other educators to do the same. She enjoys mountain biking, rock climbing, kayaking, backpacking, yoga, photography, traveling, writing, and hanging out with her family and nephews. Follow her on social media @50hikeswithkids and email wendy@50hikeswithkids.com.